730.92
Wal

171552

Waller, Irene

Textile sculp-
tures

DATE DUE

TEXTILE
SCULPTURES
IRENE WALLER

TEXTILE SCULPTURES

IRENE WALLER

WITHDRAWN

Taplinger Publishing Company
New York

First published in the United States in 1977 by
TAPLINGER PUBLISHING CO., INC.
New York, New York

Copyright © 1977 by Irene Waller

Library of Congress Catalog Card Number: 77-71688

ISBN 0-8008-7579-6

Frontispiece: Magdalena Abakanowicz
'Alterations' 1974–75 9m × 1.35m × 70cms (29′6″ × 4′5″ × 2′4½″)
A series of human forms in moulded jute fabric fibre and yarn

*'Man belongs to a world of organic structure, to its rhythms and its
rules, in contrast to the artificial world which he himself creates. The
figures emerge from my desire to demonstrate that we are a part of the
organic world. We are dependent on our organic structure, its laws
and its rhythms.
The fibre, which I use in my work, derives from plants and is similar
to that from which we ourselves are composed.'*

Contents

Introduction:
About the Fibre Art Movement   6
The History and Progress of the
Movement   8
Conclusion   13

The Work of the Following Artists:
Magdalena Abakanowicz   14
Olga de Amaral   20
Tadek Beutlich   28
Jagoda Buić   34
Barbara Chase-Riboud   42
Peter Collingwood   48
Daniel Graffin   54
Josep Grau-Garriga   60
Françoise Grossen   66
Ted Hallman   72
Sheila Hicks   78
Ritzi & Peter Jacobi   86
Gerhardt Knodel   94
Walter Nottingham   100
Wojciech Sadley   108
Moik Schiele   114
Kay Sekimachi   120
Sherri Smith   124
Inge Vahle   130
Jindřich Vohánka   136
Susan Weitzman   140
Claire Zeisler   146

Detailed Biographies   152
Bibliography   160

Introduction

The last fifteen years have seen the flowering of a new art medium, that of fibre, thread and textile-based constructions. Used by great artists to give substance to their ideas, it has resulted in some of the most significant and powerful art statements of our time.

This book is about some of these artists, and some of their greatest works.

About the Fibre Art Movement

The year 1960, although it has no significance in itself, serves well as a date by which to pinpoint the entry into full maturity of the art movement with which this book is concerned. It is the movement in which artists, some trained as painters or sculptors, and some beginning from a textile discipline, have found fibre, thread and textile-based constructions the most satisfactory and sometimes the only satisfactory medium through which they could fully express themselves. It has been slowly germinating for forty years or so and has been closely allied to movements in other art media. All have been breaking with tradition. Paintings in the 60's at first became vast and then three-dimensional, so did works in fibre. Sculpture and painting both have gone beyond the usual confines of the media and for long have used any method or material which is germane to the artist's intent—so have the works in fibre. The movement may now be said to be at its height and some of the most forceful art statements of the mid-20th century are the result.

In very simple terms, its origins lay in free experimentation on the loom by weavers of imagination. This moved outwards to include a like experimentation with other textile techniques and materials and gradually onwards until finally the expression of abstract artistic concept was fully achieved by the mastery of the use of the materials and techniques inherent in these media in a totally uninhibited, free and vigorous manner. Simultaneously, some artists trained in the 'fine art' media were searching for other means of expression. So, a wide range of artists discovered in fibre, yarn and textile-based techniques their perfect medium. They found themselves freed from both fine art traditions and the limitations hitherto dictated by the functional use of textiles. In 1974 Barbara Kasten described the stage at which the movement had then arrived as 'the marriage between fibre and dimensionality'. Certain facets of it are often called 'sculptural' and certainly part of Leroi Jones' comment about sculpture seems to apply. He says, 'Sculpture is a religious affair—this makes for a very dense object rather than a lean one. Let's call in maximal art. I think our civilisation is lean enough without underlining it. Sculpture as a created object in space should enrich . . .'. These words describe exactly the work of the great artists working in the fibre medium.

A Name

It is an art form which has long been without an adequately descriptive name. Early words like 'wall-hangings' and 'tapestries' (albeit 'new') described a technique or function, both of which are secondary to matters of form and concept. The great pieces of work are those which strike one first and foremost as overwhelming art statements, going far beyond considerations of technique. Later terms, like 'textile object', 'art fabric' and 'textile art', were loaded with reference which is still peripheral and by no means fully descriptive. The important word 'art' had been brought in but 'fabric' and 'textile' are redolent of cloth-yardage. Heckmann writes, 'Inspiration and calculation, within the creative process of experience, meditation and intuition are root notions of artistic practice'. This statement helps one to put the fibres, yarns and the textile construction, which are the language of the movement, into place. They are not of first importance in themselves, their raison d'être is that they are the material and means by which great artists are expressing their ideas.

It has already been noted that to some of the greatest of the three-dimensional work the word 'sculptural' is often applied, which would seem to indicate not only volume but total honesty of artistic intent. It seems a pity nevertheless to borrow a word which really belongs elsewhere, though we are getting very much nearer. Perhaps a new art form really needs a totally new word.

Other branches of the same general movement suffer the same problem. The words 'embroidery' and 'batik', to name but two disciplines, are totally inadequate, partly because of association, to describe the works being produced by contemporary artists who choose to employ these techniques. Luba Krejci's work, as a further instance, is firstly superb graphic imagery and secondly the lace technique.

André Kuenzi, in his *La Nouvelle Tapisserie* discourses at some length on this matter of words. I find particularly of interest his reminder to us that words are mere conveniences and that they do not have an absolute value or meaning. Words can mean different things to different people; the word 'line', for instance, will have a different meaning to a calligrapher, an electrician and a ballet dancer. Also, we must remember that over a period of time words establish a particular rapport with that which they describe and often acquire special subtle nuances. Therefore, Kuenzi suggests that to worry about words overmuch is to head for the madhouse! Nevertheless, one searches still, for words which will convey clearly to all, the lay-man and the specialist, and with no ambiguity, the nature of the art works and the art movement which we are discussing.

One thing is sure, we are talking about art and the core and essence of art is the concept, the imagery, the communication; the tools and the technique employed, however indispensable, are supportive, the hands following the dictates of the mind. Thus a descriptive phrase must reflect accurately and, for what it is worth, I have found myself, constantly, within the text, using the phrase 'the fibre art movement'. However, searching for a title for the book involved other considerations. The words 'fibre art' seemed insufficient to impart the importance and stature of the works illustrated. 'Textile Sculptures' therefore was as near as I could get, with the vocabulary available, to an evocative description of the work with which the book is concerned.

The Medium

The fact that the materials, tools and techniques are familiar, domestic and have been the means of practical fabric production throughout man's history, is both the movement's asset and its problem. Fibre is material natural to man, yarn is a use of fibre which man has invented and fabric is something that everyone uses. Fibre establishes an instant link with the natural world, of which we are an indissoluble part. It is therefore a very sympathetic medium, more immediate perhaps than pigment or stone and akin to the basic components of man himself. Because of these characteristics, extremely abstract ideas find a smooth channel of communication through this medium.

However, the medium's very familiarity leads many people with creative instincts, perhaps daunted by such uncompromising media as paint or stone, to approach techniques like crochet or knotting as well within their capabilities. One result has been avalanches of indifferent work produced under the 'art' banner. Fortunately proliferation of the mediocre does not detract one whit from the works emanating from the great artists. To see and understand the core-statements produced in the medium one must acquaint oneself with such works as Jindřich Vohánka's woven affirmations of his philosophy, Walter Nottingham's crocheted statements about nests and shrines, Magdalena Abakanowicz's woven, wound and knotted environments, Jagoda Buić's woven and pierced communications about fortresses, stones and people, or Olga de Amaral's plaited, twisted and woven walls, and many, many more. Fibre and fibre alone is the basic material which has enabled these artists to give substance to their vision.

The Artist/Craftsman Debate
Because the disciplines of painting and sculpture, as being the only accepted media for the artist, have now been questioned for so long and so basically in all areas (of which the fibre art movement is just one) artists are now using any material or technique which will give consummate substance to their thoughts, in other words, the 'fine' artist has often taken unto himself the tools and materials hitherto the province of the craftsman. Thus the distinctions between artists and craftsmen have become blurred. This has given rise to much debate on the use of the words 'artist' and 'craftsman', resulting in words like 'designer-craftsman' and 'artist-craftsman'.

Walter Gropius said, at the inception of the Bauhaus, '. . . there is no difference between the artist and the craftsman, the artist is merely a craftsman lifted to a higher plane . . .'. Now certainly he was stating something he felt very strongly in order to help rectify what had become a wide and thoroughly non-productive breach between the two—and also the statement is lifted out of context, but pondering upon it leads one to the conclusion that the aims and the motivation of the artist and the craftsman are, in fact, quite different, links between the two being mainly one of materials and methods of working. It seems reasonable to maintain that the artist's concern is to communicate abstract ideas and in order to do this he uses materials and techniques. The craftsman's concern is to produce practical objects—probably using the same materials and techniques. The blurring happens when the sheer beauty and perfection of a crafted object seems to transform it into a 'work of art' and this is where the categories 'artist-craftsman' and 'designer-craftsman' come in. So, when considering the massive output of work which is the result of the fibre art movement, it does seem important that we should recognise that there are infinite gradations of worker. There are those who are first and foremost artists, intent on conveying some concept, message or feeling, important to them and to contemporary life who will search until they find their appropriate medium, it is these who are the subject of this book. There are those whom we might call 'artist-craftsmen' whose impetus comes mainly from the material and their chosen craft but whose communication with their medium is so great and total that it becomes the means by which they transmit considerable concepts and show us new vistas. These also concern us. Then there are those whom we could call 'designer-craftsmen', (and one would hope all craftsmen fell within this category) whose mastery of their

craft is so consummate that their objects take on special virtue—as objects to contemplate as well as to use. Finally, there are those craftsmen to whom the technique is the beginning and the end and who put it to practical use only. There are also those who will plagiarize because the materials and techniques seem familiar and easy to use and there are those who are pretentious and who call forth an eminent English weaver's comment about the validity of 'taking a whacking great rope . . . copying some complicated knot out of Ashley . . . then exhibiting this large object with a "difficult" title to demonstrate its deep significance'. But these we can dismiss, their existence does not detract from the works of the great artists.

Such comments need only be made at all because of the incredible popularity that fibre and textile constructions as a medium have gained in recent years, with the consequent proliferation of fibre works and of exhibitions. There is a need for a cool appraising eye. I like very much Ed Rossbach's comment in the Constantine/Larsen book, *Beyond Craft, The Art Fabric*, 'I don't accept the distinctions between major and minor arts but I don't want to argue about it with anyone. These hierarchies become destructive. So much is destructive in our society . . .'.

The Forms
In physical terms, the work springing from the use of fibre, thread and textile constructions to non-functional ends over recent years has taken many shapes. The year 1960 was used at the beginning of this text to serve as a very general but convenient date to pin-point the coming of age of this movement, that is, an ultimate phase of freeing itself from traditionalist constraints and inhibitions. But that date represented the culmination of a struggle which was in some sense an effort to get out from under the loom—the very thing which had given the movement life—but which had to be achieved before total artistic freedom, even of the loom itself, could be arrived at. It was never a struggle for freedom from the constraints imposed by *materials,* they were always pliable, but only from the techniques which man had devised to translate the raw materials into a practical object, cloth, and which at one and the same time both inspired and inhibited.

In general terms, the first explorations of today's movement during the 1950's could be said to have been free experimentation on the loom to produce abstract statements in materials, texture and structure about physical or non-physical matters or small woven studies perhaps produced on a simple 'back strap' loom or a frame. These were very much, in terms of size, in the genre of a picture, rather the abstract and textural equivalent of a pictorial tapestry. They might even have a framing and were hung so that weaving and wall had a picture-and-wall relative relationship.

During the 60's these weavings grew into larger and more self-assertive 'statements'. Technically, they now split up, divided, grew more bulky or more transparent, owed more to the quality of the thread itself and to the forces of gravity and edges became blurred. Other techniques like warp-wrapping and weft-twining were introduced and other materials like wood, stones, glass and ceramic shapes were used. This was the era of the 'wall-hanging' which broke out of the picture frame and instead hung, making its abstract textural statements in its own way.

Some flat wall-hangings now spread outwards and were shaped peripherally, eschewing the confines of the rectangular altogether and breaking out far beyond frames or even supporting bars of any kind but still having relation in size and colour and texture to the wall which supported them. In other instances the textile statement now covered the entire wall, making the total impact, the wall being nothing but an unseen backing and, in fact, the textile acting (in a technical sense only) as some superb wallpaper. By this time the whole gamut of textile techniques was being used. Knitting and netting proved particularly amenable to shaping and cascades of of thread alone, free from any interlacement of any sort, began to be frequent elements.

Some versions of the wall-hangings now moved off the wall and into space—an important moment. They divided spaces up and created more spaces, thus making a positive physical affirmation of their own. Materials, particularly the light, the linear, the transparent, took on new meaning; silhouette and the play of light were important and work was viewed from both sides. These 'walls in their own right' became solid and more three-dimensional, and thus created entirely new walls with all the attributes of a wall but with different things to say about space and the definition of space, the treatment of surfaces and the very nature and function of walls. The new walls hung in layers or like huge leaves; they snaked in and out of themselves and each other in complex constructions, woven, wound, looped, interlaced and pierced.

At the moment when the wall-hanging was moving off the wall and into space, to act sometimes as a wall itself, so others became sculptural presences; free-standing, perhaps supported by an armature, perhaps merely supported by their own construction, or hanging, without seeming to hang, in space. Then came groups of such presences, to be walked around and viewed from every angle, with every convexity and concavity, plane and surface possible. The sculptors, some of whom had begun to work in (to them) deliberately alien soft materials and the textile constructors moving towards the firm and the free-standing, the final throwing-off of everything traditionally textile, had met another important moment.

For some artists it was logical that the body itself became the armature, thus imparting movement and life to the textile statement and bringing us back full circle to the textile's original purpose as a body-covering, but this time with what different implications. Shapes could now change from moment to moment. This idea was carried into the theatre, particularly in ballet.

Not only these body-coverings involved the body. By the 70's, along with the mainstream of artistic thought, the fibre artists now sought to involve the spectator physically—to invite him in, to touch, to move around, to partake in a total sense so that he was no longer spectator but participant. The objects took on the aspects of 'halls of mirrors', forests or canyons, labyrinths or retreats, totally enveloping environments, sometimes welcoming, sometimes menacing, nearly always huge. Some works occupied an entire gallery or moved outdoors. Some of the very latest works to have been produced seem to be concentrating attention on the human being himself rather than the menace which surrounds him. And this is, more or less, where we now stand.

The Future

It will be obvious from the illustrations that a great deal of the work produced in the last fifteen years has been, and still is, large. But, in the movement as a whole, this is not unduly meaningful. It has been the era of the architectural, the sculptural, the massive. Artists have sought to break out from the traditions long associated with fibre and yarn, that is, the closely constructed, the draped, the practical and the pictorial, and to push into the environment itself to create the very walls, the volumes and the spaces in a total and three-dimensional manner. They have sought also along the way to soften and humanise vast acres of

impersonal twentieth-century architecture and, in fact, their theme is often that of humanity and its problems. Thankfully, for their purposes, it has been a time in which materials were plentiful. But it was only an era and one in which artists were finding their way by means of the large and the monumental. The small had simply not been a valid part for a long time in the natural progression of the whole movement. But with the insistence by the great fibre artists that every inch of a piece, however gargantuan the whole, is important and individual, like a painter's brush-stroke, plus the fact that man, in general, is realising he must turn inwards, to find out what is inside, rather than constantly pushing further outwards, it has seemed recently to be the time to move closer and observe minutae and many artists have turned naturally to working on a small scale. The movement has grown its way through many forms, out of one, into another, like life itself. The matter of overall importance at this moment however is that many things have been encompassed and thus almost total freedom has been achieved for fibrous materials and textile-like treatment to be all or part of the artist's vocabulary without further constraint or limitation. As Benjamin Britten said in an address to the Aspen Institute, 'The best music to listen to in a great Gothic church is the polyphony which was written for it and was calculated for its resonance'. Ergo—in the last analysis, the size, great or small, flat or three-dimensional, of a work of art will be in direct relationship to the feeling and the spirit of the times, to the intent of its originator and to its aesthetic and practical function. One of Lenore Tawney's latest works, 'Waters above the Firmament' is, if we must label it, a wall-hanging but her thinking is not of 1960, it is timeless.

The History and Progress of the Movement

Historically, the movement could be said to stretch right back to early civilisations. Man has always found fibre, yarn and natural materials, like feathers, quills and fur, satisfying and yielding vehicles to embody his feelings about the spiritual and the eternal as well as the means of his physical comfort and protection; witness ceremonial cloaks, robes, headdresses and the like. The Middle Ages in Europe were the era of the great tapestries, when man's Christian concepts, as well as scenes of daily life, were expressed in vigorous and glowing magnificence, not in paint but in wool. This was, of course, before the 'major' and the 'minor' arts and the crafts were riven apart by the disappearance of the guilds and replaced by the academies of the Renaissance—a rift which was nearly healed in the 1930's and which may just about, in the next few decades, be closed.

The Effects of the Industrial Revolution

However, the roots of the movement as we know it now could be said to lie in the irritant qualities of the Industrial Revolution and thus were born in England. The Great Exhibition of 1851, housed in the specially-built Crystal Palace in London, was organised in order to display the products of the new machine age. What it showed clearly was that the only aesthetically truthful pieces of work were those which were products of the new technology, that is, the machines, the engines, the engineering structures, the building itself. More familiar objects, like pots, furniture and fabric, were all subjected to the new game of turning out thousands, quickly and relatively cheaply. Swiftly applied and ill-considered decoration covered everything, often out of sympathy with and totally unnecessary to the basic object and applied for reasons quite other than aesthetic. It could be done—quickly and cheaply—so why not? The artist simply didn't come into this, the only arbiter was the producer, the industrialist, the manufacturer.

William Morris and the Arts & Crafts Movement

The effect of this ugly, indigestible mass was to provoke protest from artists, poets and writers, among them John Ruskin and Edward Burne-Jones, who had themselves returned to the art of before Raphael to seek purity of image and concept. The most vocal and effective of these was William Morris an artist, poet, writer, craftsman and militant. In the 80's he preached that this total disregard for the basic and inherent qualities of materials, such as the forming of iron pillars into palm-trees, or the indiscriminate plastering of 'ornament' over everything, plus the love of quantity rather than quality, was producing monstrous mountains of junk and that a return to the simple, the basic and the honest was essential.

To achieve this, there was a return by both artists and craftsmen to hand production. They re-acquainted themselves with the basic characteristics of methods and materials and the demands of techniques and tried to observe a careful truthfulness to function and to honesty of design.

Artists and craftsmen had begun to join forces as far back as 1844 when the Art Workers Guild had been formed. After Morris founded the Arts & Crafts Movement in 1861, there was a proliferation of Arts and Crafts Societies and, in 1888, there was held the first Arts & Crafts Exhibition, which showed clearly a much healthier state of affairs.

Art Nouveau

The activities of Morris and the Arts & Crafts Societies were very much the swing of the pendulum against the excesses of the Industrial Revolution. Their response was to turn away from the machine and resort to methods of an earlier age. They did not at that point harness the machine, that was left to others who came later. There was now an effort by the arts and crafts to link with each other in order to unify into something like artistic and sociological strength. The culmination was the visually unified and international art movement known as Art Nouveau, which had a short but vigorous life, flourishing between 1890 and 1910.

One astonishing fact about Art Nouveau was that it blossomed as a truly international style, all over the Western world, under different names, but essentially the same thing. It encompassed everything, from architecture to buttons, and was characterised by clean, fluid line and close observation of nature and the human figure, albeit stylised, as a basis for flowing shape and form.

The Deutsche Werkbund and the Bauhaus

By now the machine was beginning, but only beginning, to be servant instead of master and the industrial age was achieving an intellectual maturity, one aspect of which is the ability to say no to excess and to examine the new objectively. However, the artists, the architects and the craftsmen, though influencing where they could, were still intellectually ahead of some areas of industry which, except in the totally new technologies, still clung tenaciously to outdated forms and 'applied' decoration.

In Germany, the 'Deutsche Werkbund' was formed in about 1910 as the first real and practical attempt to link art and industry. It had everything going for it as it was itself composed of both artists and industrialists and it took as its tenet the theory that the study of the applied arts and the crafts was the foundation on which to build an industry producing objects of high aesthetic and practical merit.

In 1919 the architect Walter Gropius reorganised the Weimar School of Art into the new Staatliches Bauhaus, which was a school of arts and crafts where painters, sculptors, architects, weavers, potters, jewellers all worked together, cross-fertilising each other's ideas and producing work which was indistinguishable between art and craft.

The Bauhaus Weaving School

The early weavings produced at the Bauhaus, under the influence of Paul Klee, were painterly pictorial tapestries. Later, under other instructors the weavers' attention moved outwards to embrace a wider range of textile constructions with emphasis on the structure itself, the inherent characteristics and qualities of a variety of materials, on simple and now abstract design and designing on the loom. Designing for cloth became equally important with the 'one-off' weaving and gradually designing for the power-loom together with the exploration of totally new materials, like cellophane and rayons, took total precedence. However, this time it was not the machine dictating to the artist, nor yet the artist dictating to the machine, but rather the artist using the new-found possibilities of machine power in a creative manner and in a spirit of experimentation based on respect for materials and structure. Over its lifetime the emphasis at the Bauhaus had changed, from the first painterly tapestries to concern with the intricacies of the whole field of textile construction together with a deep immersion in materials and their characteristics, finally progressing to a cool and intellectual dialogue of artist and machine, each fulfilling the demands of the other. The names of two great weavers stand out among those trained at the Bauhaus who were to have endless influence on others—Gunta Stölzl, who became weaving teacher at the Dessau Bauhaus and Anni Albers, who was to move to the USA.

The Bauhaus was closed in 1933 for political reasons and its staff and its students were scattered and spread all over the Western world, many to the States, to work and to teach. By the time of its closure, the total concern of the weaving school was with designing for industry and its impetus was such that this concept was to dominate artist-weavers for the next 25 years or more. Some of the finest production-orientated end-results were ultimately to be seen in the yardage output of the Dorothy Liebes weave studios in California and New York, the Jack Larsen New York weave studio and Alistair Morton's 'Edinburgh Weavers' in Britain. This was cloth yardage in which the emphasis lay on interesting cloth structure, innovative and sensitive use of a wide variety of materials, natural or man-made, and exuberant and sensitive use of colour; all in every gradation of cloth-weight imaginable, from the enormously bulky to the airily transparent.

Finland in the 20's, the Saarinens, and Cranbrook

In Finland, contemporary with the inception of the Bauhaus in Germany, the architect Eliel Saarinen was fulfilling one of William Morris' tenets and creating beautiful buildings, enriched with the work of specially commissioned artists and craftsmen. His wife, Loja, a weaver, had much influence on the interiors. In 1925 the Saarinens moved from Finland to the United States to create the buildings and general ambience of the Cranbrook Boys Academy, Michigan. There Saarinen followed the same pattern, commissioning artists of many skills to enrich the grounds and buildings; Swedish sculptor Carl Milles was among the greatest. Cranbrook Academy of Art, part of the complex, was founded in 1926 with Loja as head of the weaving school. Cranbrook Academy became and is one of the greatest sources of artistic creativity in the States. Like the Bauhaus, the school of weaving went through differing phases, moving from the production of hangings and rugs into concern with designing for cloth for yardage and industry and now in the 70's, very much concerned with fibre art works.

The Influence of European Artists in the United States
The Bauhaus weaving school had finally become totally preoccupied with designing for the power-loom, but its wider philosophy had an endlessly reverberating effect upon artist-weavers in general. Its influence was most directly seen in design for yardage but its philosophies very much encompassed the use of the loom as a tool for abstract creative effort. In 1933 Anni Albers and her husband, the painter and educator, Joseph Albers, moved to the United States to live, work and teach. Their precepts shaped a generation of artists, designers and teachers and through them other generations. Many other artists, craftsmen and teachers, in the ensuing years, emigrated from Europe to the States to escape suppression and very possible extinction. So, the Saarinens at Cranbrook Academy in Michigan, the Albers at Black Mountain College in North Carolina, weavers like Austrian-born Trude Guermonprez in California and the 'new Bauhaus' established in Chicago, were all to prove nerve-centres from which would spring the fibre art movement in America. These experienced artists and teachers found fertile ground in a nation whose burgeoning artists and craftsmen were unhampered by prestige-laden traditionalism but had all the richness of sources like the arts and crafts of the American Indian, of Mexico and of ancient Peru to draw upon. Bursting with creative vitality, what artists in the States needed was instruction in matters technical, but more important still, teaching and attitudes which were the product of the mainstream of European sophisticated artistic thought.

In the ensuing 40's, even in America, which was not the battleground that Europe was, artists and craftsmen were more concerned with the production of cloth yardage than with abstract creative effort. However, the war over, many men and women re-assessed the quality of life and elected to work fully as creative artists, making totally individual and personal statements, often setting up their workshops far from the cities to escape not only the noise and the dirt but also the sense of being trapped in a futile materialistic race. By the 50's, in response to this general movement with its consequent demand for education, many universities set up art departments in which widely differing materials and disciplines, not least ceramics and textiles, were seen as valid art media. To these departments artists of the highest calibre came to teach. This setting of the art departments firmly within the universities was a vital factor in determining the nature of the resulting work which was essentially personal and linked totally with the will to be an individual rather than a cog in an increasingly industrial and materialistic society. It also had a very different effect (albeit on a very different society and situation) than say in Britain, where the art colleges, the old 'Schools of Arts & Crafts', had for long remained independent and autonomous but then, in the early 70's, were one by one absorbed into the polytechnic institutions.

In very simplified terms there could by now be said to be two main centres of creativity in the States, the West and the East, each with an ambience of a very different nature. Europeans can so easily underestimate the size of the Americas and in particular the vast distance and difference between New York and San Francisco. The West Coast was and is a fertile climate for artists

and craftsmen. Ruth Asawa, a sculptress living in San Francisco, had long been producing three-dimensional, airy forms in knitted wire. Constantine and Larsen describe her work as 'America's first monumental art fabrics'. The Dorothy Liebes weave studio, though concerned with production yardage, did much to show how exciting fibre, yarn and cloth could be. The University of Berkeley in the San Francisco Bay area, where the work of the physical anthropology department greatly influenced the studies in the weaving school, was the first university to offer a Master of Fine Arts Degree in Weaving. Within its walls and under the guidance of artist-weaver, Ed Rossbach, was the training ground for many future artists. The school at Pond Farm, north of San Francisco, founded by European artist-potters, the California School of Arts and Crafts, the University of California at Los Angeles under Bernard Kester—all these centres caused California to be a breeding-ground of great creativity. Japanese-born Kay Sekimachi works there, her most unique (though not her latest) works being her airy, delicate, three-dimensional constructions in monofilament yarns. Trude Guermonprez works and teaches there, also Debra Rappoport, whose 'fibrous raiments' of the early 70's were so astonishing, Ted Hallman, Lillian Elliot, Neda Al Hilali, and others.

In the East the Cranbrook Academy of Art, of which Gerhardt Knodel is now the head, the School for American Craftsmen and the Chicago School of Design grown from the 'New Bauhaus', all flourished, producing artists of the calibre of Walter Nottingham, Claire Zeisler and the archetypal Lenore Tawney. Claire Zeisler, one of the central figures of the fibre art movement, perhaps best known for her free-standing abstract monolithic presences, lives in Chicago. Walter Nottingham, using crochet and winding as a means to create his shapes and forms, is in Wisconsin. Sherri Smith, who uses enormous and three-dimensional waffle weaves, is in Michigan.

Richard Landis is in Arizona, his austere weaving accurately reflecting the landscape, smooth surfaced and owing much to controlled cloth constructions.

Evelyn Anselevicius lives and works in Mexico. A great weaver, one of her particularly impressive forays has been to use cut pile against a contrasting ground, probably black and white, to delineate photographic-like images.

New York, of course, has never been a particularly comfortable home for artists to work in, too noisy, too busy, too concerned with fashion and the consequent obsolescence. Those who do elect to work in it must withdraw, generally down to Greenwich Village, often to the comparative calm of large airy 'lofts', former warehouses and factories. There is Lenore Tawney, whose work is a core and spirit of the movement and who in a totally detached and withdrawn manner is true *only* to her own images and thus has so often shown the way to original thinking to others. There are also Swiss-born Françoise Grossen and Mary Walker-Phillips who made such incredible contribution to progress by her innovative handling of the knit-structure. Swedish born Helena Heinmark seems to spend much of her life in the States. She uses the traditional Rosepath weave and photographic images to create vast pictorial murals.

However, New York is certainly the place in which to exhibit, midway as it is between the West Coast and Europe and being as it is the Eastern gateway to the USA. In the 1950's work was occasionally seen in the galleries, sometimes as prototypes for machine production and sometimes 'one-offs' but there was a glimmering of recognition by the mid-'50's that these were important works and indicative of something even greater to come. Jack Larsen, whose textile studio is in New York, has been a great influence in all this. The setting up of 'America House' which became the American Crafts Council with its Museum of Contemporary Crafts, was another prime factor in the recognition of the art form. There was 'Textiles USA' in 1956, 'Fabrics International' in 1960, Lenore Tawney's one-woman show in 1962 and 'Woven Forms' in 1963 at the Museum of Contempory Crafts (Tawney, Hicks, Zeisler, Adams and Zachai). Lenore Tawney was probably the one single artist responsible for making the great break-through to the public which indicated that woven forms were, in fact, art works. In 1968 the Museum of Modern Art mounted the work of eight countries in the exhibition 'Wall Hangings'. The form had truly arrived.

Britain

In the 1950's Britain and parts of Europe, because of the devastation of war, had been following a very different path from that of the United States. Emphasis was firmly placed on designing for cloth yardage. The war had brought everything to a near-end and the first concern was naturally to rebuild and re-house. Alistair Morton of Edinburgh Weavers was foremost in creating satisfying fabric and Marianne Straub and Bauhaus-trained Margaret Leischer influenced the woven textile scene greatly and, like Albers, much further than the confines of the power-loom. Ethel Mairet at Ditchling drew necessary attention to designing on the hand-loom and the important role that handweaving could play in education. At this time Britain was drawing much strength from the textile design which was then strong in Sweden.

In the early 1960's art education in Britain underwent a radical change. This brought a breath of contemporary air into the atmosphere in which students were endeavouring to design for industry but still with some of the 'sack-cloth and sandals' aura of pre-war hand-weaving. It brought about both a very realistic approach to design for the power-loom and the knitting machine and also a certain amount of freedom to experiment and make textile statements of a more abstract nature. Fuel for these latter was supplied by the exhibition 'Modern American Wallhangings' held at the Victoria & Albert Museum, London, in 1962 and the showings of work from the States and Eastern Europe in the Milan Triennale of 1964 and the Lausanne Biennales of 1962 onwards.

Tadek Beutlich and Peter Collingwood, both of whom did some teaching within the above system, emerged as Britain's two great artists in fibre in the 60's and 70's. Beutlich enjoyed the unheard-of privilege (in Britain) of having his work shown in galleries otherwise devoted to painting and sculpture, and Collingwood was accorded due honour by an exhibition with Hans Coper, the ceramist, at the Victoria & Albert Museum in 1969. Archie Brennan, Head of the Edinburgh Tapestry Company, produces his 'trompe l'œil' tapestries. Also in Edinburgh Maureen Hodge, using the tapestry weave as a base, creates three dimensional works of great impact. Ann Sutton uses tubular knits as vast warps and wefts in gigantic woven, furniture-like objects. Kathleen McFarlane uses crochet and weave to create impressive organic hangings. Robert Mabon links weave with ceramics, Theo Moorman weaves delicate graphic images in fine linen. There are other artists, and such is the excellent quality now of textile-based art education and the post-graduate work of the Royal College of Art that there will be more.

Scandinavia

In the Scandinavian countries, particularly Sweden, uninvolved with the Second World War, there had been altogether far less 'pendulum swinging' than in Britain and Europe. Their long-standing, firmly-rooted, craft tradition had remained strong and healthy despite the Industrial Revolution and perhaps also their comparative geographical remoteness was of help. They had embraced and used the new technology rather than be swamped by it. New attitudes and styles were gently absorbed while the output of beautiful hand-crafted objects continued un-broken and remained a steadying and inspiring influence on machine production, there often being no discernible difference, between hand and machine-produced goods. Märta Mäas Fjetterström was the towering influence in the 30's and 40's, producing carpets, rugs and hangings, strong, robust and uncompromising and rooted totally in the native craft and ambience of Sweden. In the 50's the work of the Swedish artist. Ulla Tolluf, and the Finnish artists, Eva Antilla and Marta Taipale, incorporated threads and graphic images with sensitivity and freedom. Finnish Dora Jung designed in a totally free graphic way for the Jacquard loom, just as Alistair Morton was doing in England.

France and Switzerland

Simultaneously with all these happenings, something yet different again had happened in France. In 1939 the painters Lurçat, Gromaire and Dubreuil had applied themselves to study the design and production of tapestry at the Gobelin and Beauvais factories at Aubusson. Tapestries had degenerated to the flat and lifeless. The participation of the painters, particularly that of Jean Lurçat, was to revolutionise French tapestry. It was to remain flat but now artists designed with tapestry in mind and the results were objects of glowing, pictorial impact, totally contemporary in feeling, depicting the main-stream of art momentum but comparative in weave-relevance to the Medieval tapestries. Tapestries now became known as 'murals'. In 1962, at Lurçat's instigation, the first Biennale de la Tapisserie was organised in Lausanne, Switzerland, by the Centre International de la Tapisserie Ancienne et Moderne, basically in order to give showings to this revival of the French tapestry art. But the Biennale's committee was nothing if not forward and outward-looking and included also were some revolutionary fibre art works, mainly from Eastern Europe, which could not have been more unlike in execution, though not in some of their concepts, the French tapestries, sometimes their main element in common being size! Since then the Lausanne Biennales have been the foremost occasions at which there is opportunity to see some of the latest developments in the fibre art movement.

Several of the great artists are based in Paris. Included in the Biennales almost since their inception has been the work of Sheila Hicks who lives in Paris, and whose handling of thread as thread and as skeins and cascades of thread is masterly. Her work and influence stretches far and wide. Pierre Daquin was one of the first traditionally-trained tapestry artists to break its chains, his 'Cage du Vent' being shown at the fifth Biennale. Working now in Paris after a period in the south, is the, until recently, little known, but a giant already, Daniel Graffin. The Afro-American sculptress, Barbara Chase-Riboud incorporates thread in her works of cast bronze with seeming inevitability. Marc Bankowsky's three-dimensional work shown in 1975 at Lausanne, takes the form of a netted hemisphere, mounted on scaffolding and placed out of doors as a plaything. In Southern France works Swiss-born

Marguerite Carau-Ischi. Her material is mainly sisal, her colours cool and neutral to gently sunny and her imagery distilled simplicity itself.

Meantime in Switzerland the great artist/weaver and teacher, Elsi Giauque, had for long been making seminal contribution to foremost thinking in the fibre art movement—a conceptualist of the finest order. Many of her works were to be the first of their kind as well as the springboard for the minds of others and have been exhibited at almost all the Biennales. Her 'Spatial Elements' shown in Amsterdam in 1969 were a series of metal rectangular frames wound with fine thread alone, interlacing was minimal. The frames occupied space in a totally dominating manner. These were to astonish all and to free many artists of the domination of the wall but, in fact, Giauque had been thinking in this manner twenty years before! The originator of many of the 'break-throughs', her flat, framed weavings glow and vibrate like paintings, her use of proportion, colour and texture masterly. She was the student of painter Sophie Taeuber-Arp at the École des Arts et Métiers, Zurich, who, in an era when it was still strange to do so, had expressed many of her concepts in, of all things, cross-stitch embroidery and other textile techniques. Giauque was to become head of textiles at the school until 1965.

Swiss-born and trained Françoise Grossen was to move to the United States. Moik Schiele, in Zurich, a pupil of Giauque's, creates both the flat and the three-dimensional, the large and the minute, with equal strength. Marlise Stahelin creates solid dense objects and Ann-Mari Matter objects in which the warp is left almost undisturbed by occasional weft picks.

Germany and Holland

In Germany, the Roumanian-born Jacobis create works of incomparable presence, often concerned with landscape. Inge Vahle's murals deal with menace and mechanisation. Eva and Wilhelm Heer construct their 'play objects', large or small, rope or fibre objects, the aesthetic and practical elements of which are inseparable. Brunhild El Attar produces space objects. In the work of Sophie Dawo we are confronted with vast areas of originally conceived texture. In the Netherlands, Wilhelmina Fruytier creates tapestries which are direct, enormous in scale and immediate, their main element being a tapestry weft of heavy rope. She works for architectural spaces and her tapestries are an integral part of the space which they occupy, with the same massive feel as the components of the building itself. In Holland also Herman Scholten weaves his convoluted yet flat tapestries with eccentric wefting; Harry Boom produces clear plastic walls, each 'thread' being a wide strip of clear plastic. Loes van der Horst in her career as weaver has made a total change from the use of natural materials and figurative images to something quite different—the exclusive use of synthetic materials making, as the materials demand, new forms concerned and integrated totally with the world of today.

Spain

The Catalan ateliers of Sant Cugat del Valles near Barcelona were established in 1945, to produce tapestries. Josep Grau-Garriga studied the French tapestry revival under Lurçat and now directs the atelier in the production of contemporary work, totally of today yet rooted in the local landscape and ambience.

Also in Catalonia work French-born Maria Thérèse Codina and Aurelia Muñoz, both formidable artists indeed. Codina experiments with the use of natural light, air, space, her weavings live in space. Muñoz works much in sisal in a variety of

techniques but often macramé to produce solidly-built, dense, three-dimensional geometric objects.

Also to the same area has now gravitated Polish-born Tadek Beutlich from Britain.

Eastern Europe

Simultaneously with Britain's post-war preoccupation with cloth yardage, in Eastern Europe, even more ravaged, something quite different had happened which would be similar in result to things happening in the United States, though arrived at by a totally different route. Poland, Czechoslovakia and Yugoslavia, in pre-war times, all had strong and flourishing local handweaving traditions and very fine schools of weaving. After the war the governments saw fit to rebuild and encourage these and to encourage and support artists in general. Much cross-fertilisation occurred between artists in all media to result, among the weavers, in the most incredible upsurge of vigorous, uninhibited, artistic statements, absolutely germane to the state man found himself in and forceful beyond words in their strength and impact. The very basic format and discipline of tapestry weaving was seen taken to its ultimate limits, deeply textured, pierced, shaped and accruing unto itself any textile material or construction which served its ends but always with meaning, with care, with respect. Here was a well-spring indeed of the new movement owing nothing to anyone, a very source itself.

Poland had a flourishing tapestry art in the 16th, 17th and 18th centuries, which the dissolution of the social structure and then the Industrial Revolution had destroyed. In the early 20th century two establishments for the arts were set up, the Association of Polish Applied Art and the Cracow Workshops but these were destroyed by World War 1. In 1926 a co-operative society of artists, L.A.D., concerned themselves with the resuscitation of Polish weaving and during the 30's Mieczyslaw Szymanski produced about ten enormous tapestries incorporating other techniques, such as embroidery and pile. There were many fine artists giving substance to their creative imagination through the medium of weaving at that time. Intellectual thought plus the manipulation of colour, fibres and mixed techniques were inseparable. Again a war destroyed everything—or nearly everything, though in Cracow Helen and Stefan Gralkowski managed to keep tapestry weaving going. After the war there was a revival of artistic life, the flames of which were perhaps fanned by the very experience of total destruction and therefore the opportunity for basic rebuilding and re-thinking. The Polish Ministry of Art and Culture caused local handicrafts, particularly weaving, to be set up anew. The centre of tapestry weaving moved from Cracow to Warsaw where Academies and Schools of Fine Arts and experimental workshops opened. Polish art education was re-organised. By about 1956 something revolutionary started to happen. In the new structure, emphasis has been placed on much inter-relation between the various art disciplines plus sound basic studies on materials and techniques. Those artists who had chosen fibre and woven techniques as their medium began to make statements of astonishing originality and force. These were rooted in the artists' communion with the loom, with a variety of techniques and with the inherent characteristics of the raw materials. Work 'came off the wall', became a three-dimensional form using many materials, wood, fur, rope, leather; it became an integral part of architectural space.

Since then, to quote Danuta Wroblewska, 'Polish weaving has held the centre of world attention'. It was first seen in about 1957 at the Milan Triennale and at the 1962 Lausanne Biennale it had a forceful showing when it amazed all, delighting some and enraging others. The work of five artists was shown, Magdalena Abakanowicz, Jolanta Owidzka, Wojciech Sadley, Ada Kierzkowska and Anna Sledziewska, all working in the most forceful, vigorous and dominating manner. Abakanowicz, who is undoubtedly the giant and whose monumental and elemental work is always at the spearhead of advancement, works in direct colours on vast sculptural forms composed of massive wefts of sisal and jute. Sadley works with softer, pendulous, sometimes transparent forms in netting or weaving. Owidzka's large works were generally flat and rectangular compositions of light and dark texture and pattern. Zofia Butrymowicz creates large murals and panels in hand-spun vegetable-dyed wools. Her works have the look of paint applied with a thickly loaded brush and yet owe everything to weaving. Barbara Falkowska creates flat tapestries in which flowers, plants and stones are her images, invested with a timeless quality by her use of yarn, shape and colour which speak of both now and of the world's beginning. Ursula Plewka-Schmidt is one of the younger weavers and a pupil of Abakanowicz who creates large, free-standing concave and convex forms in knitting or similar techniques stretched on willow, the whole on an armature of metal, works of immense size and presence and somehow privateness. Not least, are Luba Krejci's graphic statements using the lace technique in either a flat or three-dimensional manner.

Jindřich Vohánka, Bohdan Mrazek and Jiri Tichy, the three great Czech artist/weavers, all work on shaped weavings which have enormous philosophical and visual impact. The works are generally flat and have this much in common with traditional tapestry but there it ends. Warp and wefts are moved out of place to disappear or to create new areas; edges of works owe nothing to the rectangular or to selvedges. Other equally well-known Czech weavers are Jan Hladik, Jarmila Cihankova and Brit Warsinski.

Yugoslav artist, Jagoda Buić, another giant, weaves her fortresses and her 'personages'. Her work is in galleries world-wide and confronted with it one is silenced. It is the ultimate in three-dimensional visual statements.

Eastern Europe is indeed a fountain-head of the fibre art movement.

East and West Come Together
It was not until the 1960s, mainly through the Milan Triennale of 1964, the Lausanne Biennales from 1962 onwards and exhibitions in Amsterdam, Madrid and Paris, that Western Europe and the world in general became fully aware of the exciting things which were happening as far apart as the States and Eastern Europe, in the use of fibre and yarn and textile-like constructions to an abstract end. There, in the American Pavilion of the 1964 Milan Triennale, Europe saw for the first time Lenore Tawney's shaped and pierced floor to ceiling 'King', 'Queen' and 'River' tapestries and her 'Hammock', Dominic di Mare's three-dimensional weaving and, not least, Mary Walker-Phillips' outstanding innovations in the use of knitting. There from Eastern Europe, in the Lausanne Biennales, was Luba Krejci's graphic use of the lace technique and, among many other Eastern European artists' work, Magdalena Abakanowicz's incredible woven 'walls' and the work of Sadley, Buić, Vohánka and others. Thus from East and West came strong, forceful, mature statements of the fibre art movement brought together with the work of Western Europe and shown at one after another of impressively-mounted exhibitions in the great galleries of Western Europe and in North and South America.

Further Afield
The borders of the fibre movement stretch ever further and further. The Colombian artist Olga de Amaral has been for long central to the movement and has her studio in Bogotá. Sculptress Alicia Penalba who now works with fibre lives in Argentina, Mariette Rousseau-Vermette, in Quebec, produces entire wool-textured walls intended to bring the feeling of the Canadian landscape outside, to the inside. Polish-born Ewa Jarosynzka and Mona Hessing both work in Australia. The Japanese artists also entered the field a few years ago and one waits with interest to see where their work will go. At the 1975 Lausanne Biennale there was a Russian exhibit.

Conclusion

From the foregoing hopefully there has emerged a picture—an outline of the growth of the movement into the world-wide art form that it has become, with indication of the infinite variety of work produced by some of the many artists who are practising today.

We saw that from Britain and the irritant of the Industrial Revolution at its source, through the reactions of the critics as given voice by William Morris, there ultimately evolved, in Europe, that power-house of basic thought the German Bauhaus. The closure of the Bauhaus caused the dissemination of its thinking via its staff and students, all over Europe and to the United States. This was one limb of the movement. Another was the upsurge in the '40s and '50s of seminal artistic creative activity by State-encouraged artists in Eastern Europe, notably Poland and Czechoslovakia, both of which had had everything but the spirit of life itself crushed out of them repeatedly by war. Coming from such different sources these were brought together in the 1960's in great and superbly presented exhibitions in the museums of Western Europe and in New York, thus showing the world, in toto, what was happening. From there on the movement has spread ever further and the use of fibre, thread and textile-based methods of construction as an art medium is now a fully-recognised and world-wide movement.

To do adequate justice to such a subject would have taken a book of encyclopaedic proportions, so it was necessary to limit one's objectives. I decided, therefore, to confine the area of concentration to where the movement is today and to focus in on a comparatively few artists in order to be able to get inside what they are doing though where it has seemed important an artists earlier key works may well have been included.

The visual arts communicate in their own terms and need few words to justify them, indeed it could be said that if words are needed then the work has failed. Comment on the works themselves therefore has been limited. Where I have been able, however, to prevail upon an artist to make comment upon their work as a totality, I have seized upon and included such comments with great satisfaction as *their* words about their thought processes cannot be improved upon. We are fortunate indeed to be given an insight into the richess of their imaginations and the workings of their minds. I have tried to outline each artist in not too many words; detailed biographies are placed right at the end of the book.

There is only one further thing to say and it is directed to the artists included—my gratitude to them for their participation in the book, necessitating as it did effort on their part in assembling information, is outstripped only by my admiration for their work.

Magdalena Abakanowicz

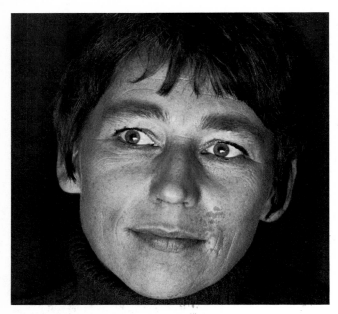

Magdalena Abakanowicz is Polish and was born in Falenty in 1930. She is undoubtedly among the very greatest of the artists working with the textile media today. Her studio is in Warsaw and she is married to a civil engineer.

She studied painting and sculpture at the Fine Art Academy in Warsaw from 1950 to 1955 and for the six ensuing years she worked in the media in which she had been trained. The period of her studentship and early years as an artist was an era of great artistic turbulence and ferment as restraints which had been imposed since the war were slowly giving way and the dammed-up energy of the creative came spilling over. In about 1962 she turned to weaving and the use of fibre and yarn as a technique and materials more capable of transmitting her overwhelming concepts with the desired force. She weaves directly with her fingers, interlacing the yarn into the warp without aid of shuttles or harnesses, mainly because her involvement is with every inch of the work and repetition of any sort has no part in her thinking. This total physical involvement between herself and her work is all the more incredible when one realises that the materials with which she works are monstrous and the scale of her works vast, seeming as big as cathedrals and as enveloping as coal mines. In fact, this analogy is particularly apt because the effect of her work is to awe, envelope and involve the spectator in the manner of great architecture or natural phenomena.

In every undertaking she dominates the situation totally. Not for her the placing of a hanging on a wall—she would rather create the wall itself, and not for her mere participation in an exhibition, she would rather structure the exhibition entire. For this forcefulness and domination we can only be grateful to her because her imagery and artistic statements are without equal.

She and her work are internationally familiar. She exhibits and takes part in textile 'happenings' all over the world. Her work is in galleries and buildings world-wide and is illustrated in every major book or work concerned with fibre and yarn as the artist's media.

In 1965 she was given the award of the Biennale of Art at Sao Paulo. She has been honoured numerous times by her own country and in 1974 she was given a Degree of Doctor honoris causa of the Royal College of Art, London. Since 1965 she has taught at the Academy of Fine Arts, Poznan, where she is now professor.

'When I talk about my work I know that I can only touch on a few of its many aspects.

Every form has its origin in intuition and its contact with the external world.

I have often felt that hand-woven fabric is not taken very seriously because it has been a part of our civilisation from the very beginning. Before becoming an element of decoration or a tapestry emulating the art of painting, it was quite modestly a protective covering for man.

It is essential for me to reveal those very aspects of the woven material, in my own work. I started to construct it into three-dimensional forms by sewing them together like garments or tents. I made them on such a scale that people could enter

inside them and touch the surfaces. As in nature, every square inch of a hand-woven surface is different from the next one.

My intention was to extend the possibilities of man's contact with a work of art through touch and by being surrounded by it.

I have looked to those slowly growing irregular forms for an antidote against the brilliance and speed of contemporary technology. I wanted to impose a slower rhythm on the environment as a contrast to the immediacy and speed of our urban surroundings.

In my exhibitions, I have tried to make rhythms of forms in space with woven objects and ropes, and lead the spectator through a sequence of effects and impressions. My exhibitions are prepared a long time in advance. I study the available space and then make arrangements of forms and objects in such a way as to achieve the maximum interplay between them, the space and the light. An area which is arranged in this way becomes a work of art in its own right. The best analogy with what I am trying to do is music, which in a given room is all pervasive and which at the same time reflects the space which contains it.'

Magdalena Abakanowicz
Statement made at the time of the Whitechapel Art Gallery Exhibition, 1975

Detailed biography on page 152

'Abakan Orange' 1971

(See also frontispiece, 'Alterations')

'Abakan Black Round', 'Abakan Black Great' 1971, exhibited at the Pasadena Art Museum

Right: 'Deviation' 90cm × 150cm (3′ × 5′)

Previous page: 'Relief in Space' 21.3m × 7.2m (71′ × 24′) 1971. Black and brown sisal and wool shaped weavings with other techniques. Commissioned for a reception room of a State Building at S'Hertogenbosch, Netherlands

Olga de Amaral

Olga de Amaral is Colombian and was born in Bogotá, the capital, in 1932. She is married to painter Jim Amaral, is head of the Estudio Amaral in Bogotá, and has until recently been the only internationally acclaimed fibre artist to come from South America.

She studied architecture at the Colegio Mayor de Cundinamarca in Bogotá from 1951 to 1953 and this influence shows clearly in her textile works. She then studied textiles at Cranbrook Academy of Art, Michigan from 1954 to 1955. From 1960 she began to exhibit, at first mainly in South America, then in South and North America, then also in Europe until now her work is shown world-wide, including Australia. In 1963 she became Director of Architectural Design and in 1966 Director of Textiles at the Universidad de los Andes in Bogotá. In 1970 she opened her own studio-shop. The body of the studio is concerned with producing hand-woven upholsteries and carpets. From this practical and organised basis Olga de Amaral builds her own particular creative imaginings, her 'woven walls'. Her early weavings had been small studies but gradually grew in size and concept until her works became compact, strong, forceful, often free-standing, intricate interlacings of tapestry-woven or wrapped vertical strips, crossing, re-crossing and mingling with each other to create three-dimensional interplay of plane and colour.

Her work is in public buildings and public and private collections in North and South America and is featured in all major works on textile art. She has had innumerable one-man and shared exhibitions, possibly the first most important being her one-man exhibition in New York in 1970 and her constant showing at the Lausanne Tapestry Biennales since 1967. In 1973 she was awarded a Guggenheim Fellowship and this resulted in a period spent living and working in Paris during 1974 and 1975.

As visiting artist, she instructs at various colleges and universities in the United States and participates in conferences. From 1968 to 1972 she was Colombia's representative to the World Crafts Council and from 1970 has been Director for the Latin American section of the World Crafts Council.

Constantine and Larsen call her 'the most dynamic force in the Americas and a prodigious artist' and this seems very fair comment. Her work is deep and vast in conception. The influence of her early architectural training can be clearly seen as her 'walls' divide and occupy space with sculptural and organic presence. Contemplation of them suggests to the onlooker that Olga de Amaral is assisting nature invent new forms of growth.

Interestingly, an invitation to participate in an exhibition of small textile objects recently has, slightly to her own surprise, led her to move very decisively from the large back to the small. This was demonstrated clearly and forcibly in her exhibition at the Rivolta Gallery in Lausanne which coincided with the 7th Biennale. These works are totally different from her 'walls' in that instead of settling into a total architectural conception, they are more like paintings—small, concentrated, jewel-like statements (though often using the techniques and elements of the walls, in miniature), framed and boxed. Hanging at eye level, they take the onlooker into the heart of themselves, coolly stated, golden, glowing, fibrous and intricate. Whether large or small, her work reflects completely the aura that emanates from Olga de Amaral herself, calm, quiet, content, absolute master of her creative will and means and totally in communication with the people and the world around her.

'Even though, as has occasionally happened, Olga de Amaral might produce small format works, the scale of her tapestries is always magnificent. The proportional relationship between component elements suggests a great ability to embrace space. This is due in part to the materials and their behaviour under the action of light and in part to the way in which the structure of the tapestry forces it to hang.

Olga de Amaral works with two different types of fibre, horse hair and virgin wool. The horse hair is almost always dyed and displays its hardness, resiliency and, above all, iridescence by the reception and reflection of light. On the other hand, the muted tones of virgin wool serve to bring out and, at the same time, to keep under control the colours and the strength of the horse hair.

As far as hanging is concerned, these tapestries are put together in such a way that when they abandon the loom they lose the plane upon which they had been built. They are designed to work by weight and counterweight, as dynamic structures in which the consistency of one part is opposed to that of another, so as to create tense balances and dramatic gestures. Here weight produces form, as in gothic vaults and flying buttresses. The complex form that the tapestry achieves under the action of weight is accentuated by its two faces (for it emerges two-sided from the loom) so as to create a sculptural figure.

It is not strange that Olga de Amaral's works should make reference to architecture since part of her early education related to that field. This helps explain the intellectual will, located at the origin of these forms, as a determination to modify space without competing with architecture, and evading decorative embellishment. The point located between the architectonic and supportive elements is hard to establish and is one of the constant stimuli upon the conception of her work. Eventually this point is referred to as the possibility of integrating the tapestry with the place in which it shall exist. It should be kept in mind, however, that de Amaral works without knowing the places where her pieces will eventually

hang. In the great majority of cases she conceives them as easel works which are conceptually transportable, this meaning that their design allows them to adapt to the multiple situations they might find. Because of all this, the tapestries have defined their plastic condition by progressively achieving the transparent state. But it should be kept clear that the transparency referred to, far from meaning the physical condition of not interrupting vision, implies the aesthetic capacity for allowing the perception of space.

As mirrors would allow, or gold, or any object treated with the camouflage technique, like that master at such discipline, the chameleon (or, for that matter, any plant or animal when it exists, with its vital vibration, among its kindred) these are the aims of de Amaral's tapestries. They occur as works of art that have managed to obtain relative invisibility and have clarified their will not to be observed directly, nor of being focused on, nor of becoming the focal point of the spatial set-up, but of giving form, though only partially, to the backgrounds and their surroundings.'
Galeor Carbonell
This statement is the result of a dialogue between Olga de Amaral and Galeor Carbonell, the Colombian art critic.

Detailed biography on page 152.

'Estructure de un parraje' 1972 3m × 2m (9′10″ × 6′7″) Green, grey and grey-pink horsehair and wool; weaving, winding and interlacing

'Coraza en des Colores' 1971 4m × 1.6m (13′11″ × 5′3″) Orange and pink horsehair and wool
Right: **Detail of 'Coraza en des Colores'**

'Dusky Stripes' 137cm × 87cm (4′4″ × 2′11″) Horsehair and wool, yellow, white pink; woven

Left: 'Coraza en Elementus Naturales' 2.5m × 1m (8′4″ × 3′3″)

'Complete Fragment' 1975 Linen, wool, horsehair, gesso

Above left: 'Complete Fragment' 1975 Linen, wool, horsehair, gesso
Left: 'Complete Fragment No 12' 1975 45cm × 30cm (1′6″ × 1′) Horsehair and gesso

Tadek Beutlich

Tadek Beutlich was born in Lwowek in Poland in 1922. He studied art in Poland, in Germany and in Italy, concerning himself with drawing and painting.

In 1947 he moved to England and attended the Sir John Cass School of Art for a year. One year later he began to weave, having seen the exhibition of French tapestries at the Victoria and Albert Museum, London, and been inspired and fascinated by them and by watching the French weavers at work. As there was no weaving taught at the Sir John Cass School, he moved to Camberwell School of Art, where he was taught by Mrs Drew and later Barbara Sawyer. From 1951 to 1974 he taught and lectured at the school. In 1967 he moved into 'Gospels', once the Sussex studio of that earlier great weaver, thinker and writer, Ethel Mairet and for many years Britain was proud to claim him as one of her great artists in fibre.

In 1967 he published *Technique of Woven Tapestry*. In this book he was one of the first to bring to general notice the validity of fibre and yarn and the woven technique as an art medium. In it points are often illustrated by his own early work. A review of the book commented that his works are 'intimations of immortality' which indeed they are. They have changed in style and technique over the years, from a delicacy of handling and materials with the accent on fine thread and transparency, to a monumentality in scale, handling and concept. Always the underlying theme seems to be about the eternal, albeit using the moon, landscape and natural and insect forms as the vehicle. Present large works are often seamed to achieve areas of concavity which add emphasis to massive cascades and twists of heavy, unspun sisal or jute.

He has exhibited regularly in galleries devoted to sculpture since 1963 in Britain and internationally and his hangings are illustrated in all major works on fibre-art. In 1973 he moved from England to Spain where he now lives and works.

Detailed biography on page 152.

'Eruption' 1970 280cm × 325cm (9′4″ × 10′10″) Red and black unspun sisal and jute

Left : 'Bird of Prey' 3.66m × 1.52m (12′ × 5′) Sisal

Above: '**Moonworshipper**' *Right:* '**Roots**' Overtwisted wool *Far right:* '**Arcangel I**' 1971 (detail) 260cm × 250cm (8′7″ × 8′3″) Plain weave; sisal and mixed fibres bleached white

'Dawn' 1974 20cm × 20cm (8″ × 8″) Sisal and jute

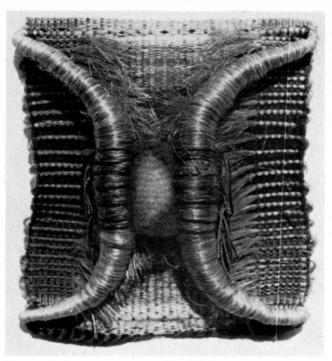

'Sunset' 1974 20cm × 20cm (8″ × 8″) Sisal and jute

'Little Moon' 1974 20cm × 20cm (8″ × 8″) sisal, jute and paper

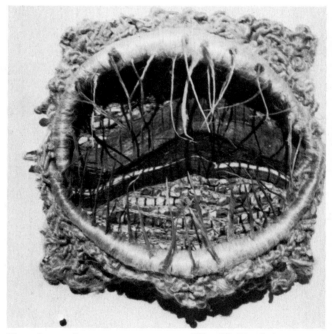

'Landscape' 1974 20cm × 20cm (8″ × 8″) Sisal, jute, paper and wool

'Undercurrent' Jute and sisal

Jagoda Buić

Jagoda Buić is Yugoslavian and was born in Split, Dalmatia, in 1930. She works in Zagreb, in Dubrovnik and sometimes in Paris.

Her works are monumental and without peer. They fill one with awe and seem to feed one's spirit with their grandeur, beauty and strength. They are the product of an artist who is steeped in the painting, the applied arts, the ambience and the terrain of her own and surrounding countries and whose work is affected by her deep love for the theatre.

Her father's concern with the arts and his contact with many great painters of Yugoslavia were her very earliest influences. In 1949 she entered the University of Zagreb to study the History of Art. From there she went to Italy to study, to travel and to work with costume and decor at Cinécitta. In 1953 and 1954 she studied tapestry and theatre decor at the Academy of Applied Arts, Vienna. While there, she was awarded a major prize, executed a decor for the theatre at Schoenbrunn and, on her return to Yugoslavia, produced costumes and decor for the ballet, the opera and for Shakespearean productions, collecting more major awards the while.

From then on, her movements became world-wide — Italy, Scandinavia, Switzerland, France, Germany, Holland, Denmark, Britain, Canada, the States and South America — to take a major part in exhibitions (every Lausanne Biennale except the first), projects and textile

happenings. Her involvement with tapestry became greater and total and her works even more forceful and impressive, both in impact and in their deep effect upon the senses. Awards came thick and fast and she became recognised as among the top four or five of the world's great artists working with the textile medium.

Her work has already been described as having grandeur, beauty and strength. Always they occupy space with immense presence and evoke emotions about things like fortresses, places, people, situations and ideas. She does this by means of weave themes like herring-bones and twills, produced on a gigantic scale, in jutes, wools, and sisals, always in sombre, dark colours, lit by occasional glints of gold or shiny dark threads and illuminated by the effect of light on the three-dimensionality of the weaves. The works are pierced, concave and convex, they hang, they stand, they hover, they brood. Needless to say, they are illustrated in innumerable catalogues and in all serious books on artists using the textile medium.

She is warm, totally without pretention, indefatigable and as an artist unsurpassed.

'Everything starts with thread. In the legend of Ariadne Theseus found the way out of the labyrinth by means of a thread—thread being the symbol of intelligence.

For me, weaving has always been the medium with the greatest potential. Everything is done by construction, the very basis and essence of weaving. Modern tapestry can be of two kinds, it can be a structure with surfaces formed by warp and weft, or it can integrate with architectural space. In its traditional form tapestry is like a wall, a defence against infinity. Since a wall is also a bulwark against fear it contains itself all the elements of fear. Therefore it is that which it resists. It is inhuman. One does not touch a wall. It is not tactile, but cold and flat. The wall endeavours to acquire a soul of its own in many ways. One way was the portrayal of events in everyday life seen in medieval tapestries. The wall, when it was composed of such incontestable ingredients, became important.

However tapestry lost its story telling role. It became instead a copy of paintings and condemned to be mere decoration.

In the new tapestries however, imaginary structures are created by the composition and arrangement of shapes. This form of tapestry gives imaginary values visual form. It does not imitate visual ideas, it expresses things psychical and physical. The intellectual developments resulting from the interlacing of threads, the tactile quality of tapestry, the intimate eroticism of warm and flexible surfaces make certain shapes and patterns happen which create new forms. I project these forms into space. This way, the material has an integrity of its own.

Three-dimensional tapestry represents a liberation from traditional discipline. It finds its absolute justification in modern architecture, in spaces no longer dominated by walls

'Flexions Continuité' and other works, Musée d'Art Moderne, Paris 1975

but by windows. The weaving takes on the qualities of a wall existing independently in space.

The characteristic that my work has in common with sculpture is its three dimensionality, and with painting, its surface textures.

All my efforts until now, in the breaking up of the surface plane of weaving, have led me further into the exploration of structure and materials. In 1966 I made my first spatial tapestry. It was the result of such important thought-processes that I even built a round loom. This experience in space and structure led me to new conceptions and into a meditative silence. Liberated from and beyond innovation I felt that at last I was penetrating into the essence of a pure act of creation.

I ask myself whether the things which are happening around us today are not indicative that we are in the middle of a crisis of sensibility? Perhaps the new tapestries could be the means of bringing fresh ideas to a plasticised world. Tapestry has gone far beyond its original potential and has taken on the characteristics of a different medium.

But perhaps one should not dissect one's work so much. In a work of art it is the work alone which matters.'
Jagoda Buić, 1975
Exhibition 'Formes Tissées', Musee de l'Art Moderne, Paris.

Detailed biography on page 153.

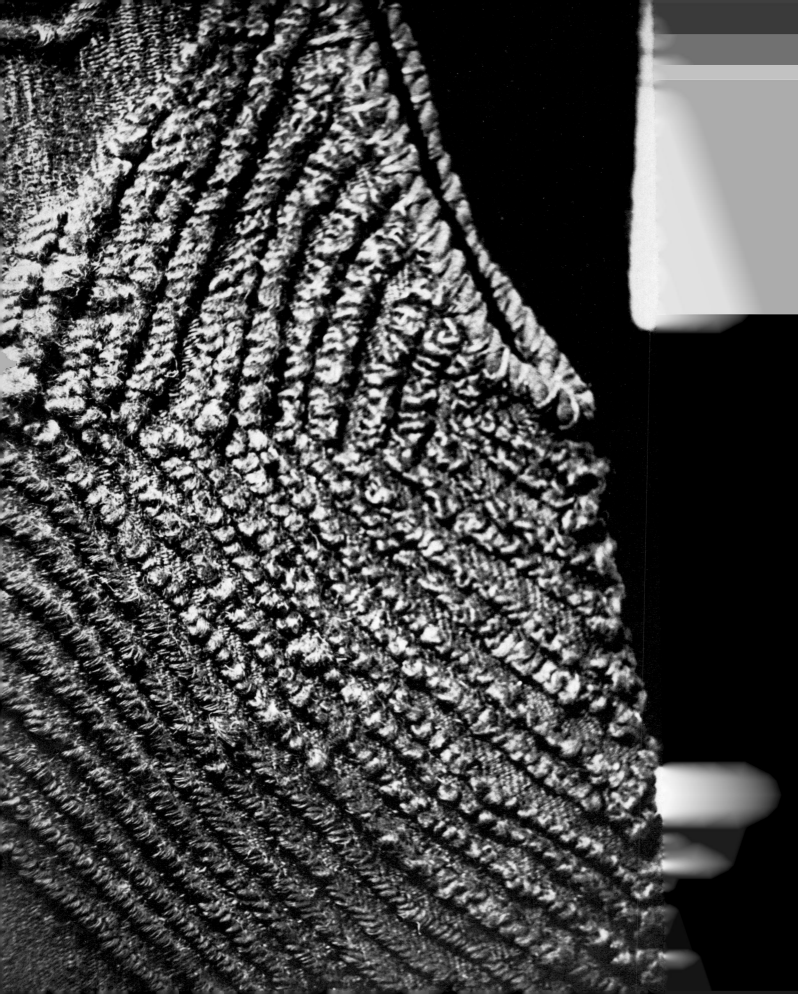

Left: '**Personnages de Macbeth**' 1973

Below: '**Trace Noir**' 1969 Three dimensional black woven formes; jute, sisal and wool

Far left: '**Personnages de Macbeth**' (detail) Three-dimensional shaped and pierced woven forms, with other techniques; black jute, wool and sisal

'Variabil Noir' (detail)

Right: **Part of 'Structure Noir' 1969 Three-dimensional shaped and pierced woven forms, with other techniques; black jute, wool and sisal**

'Variabil Noir' 1974–75 3.5m × 6m × 1m (12′ × 20′ × 3′4″) A group of woven forms in black and glints of gold and bronze; sisal, jute and wool

Barbara Chase-Riboud

Barbara Chase-Riboud is American-Canadian, of African descent.

One discerns both contemporary America and ancient Africa in her work. Sculptor, draftsman and poet, she was born in Philadelphia, Pennsylvania, in 1939. She was educated at the Tyler School of Fine Arts of Temple University and was awarded its outstanding alumni award in 1975. She received a John Hay Whitney Fellowship in Sculpture to study in Rome, Italy, and completed her studies at the Yale University School of Art and Architecture (MFA) in 1960.

It was at Yale, studying under Rico Lebrun and Josef Albers, that she first met Sheila Hicks who was to be a great friend and to whom she turned to for advice when she began her continuing series of metal sculptures incorporating silk, wool and fibres.

At the end of a seven year retirement, after completing a large-scale fountain in Washington D.C. in 1960, her installation in Paris, France in 1961 and numerous trips to India, North Africa and especially China in 1965 that she turned from her surrealist lost-wax bronzes to her first major series of combined-material sculptures: 'Four Monuments to Malcolm X'. Although she was completely disengaged from the 'Pop' movement of her contemporaries of the 60s, the ensuing breakdown of traditional materials

for art objects, and the introduction of 'self-destroying' (as in Tinguely) and non-permanent materials (Oldenburg) set her free to explore new techniques, specifically the incorporation of rope, cord, plait and knot form, synthetics, wool and hemp into cast bronze reliefs. The purpose was twofold; a technical one, to eliminate the need for a base or surrealistic 'legs' which she felt distracted from the emotional impact of the sculptures by framing or referring them and, secondly, to enhance the intensity of the form by attaching it in a concrete way to the floor or wall so that it becomes an organic and independent 'personage' or entity much in the context, but in an entirely different manner as Anthony Caro's base-less steel structures. A totally contemporary concept on one hand is fused with a time-less and almost science-fiction monumentality and primitive magic.

Her technical competence and attention to finish is an important element in both sculptures and drawings. The latter are of stones, bones, rocks and fissures which almost always, though they *appear* to have been drawn directly from nature, are transformed metaphysically by incorporating bindings, skirts, wrappings or loops of meticulously drawn cords or 'automatic' imaginary writing which sometimes includes verses of poetry. Her theme is always the combination of opposites: time and eternity, mathematics and poetry, the personal and the cosmic, force and tenderness, male and female, shadow and light. In one word, her work is about interpenetration and she achieves it by the handling of two conflicting materials as in the sculptures or two conflicting contexts as in the drawings. Each material is left with its own majesty, but also confers upon the other something of itself; the metal has a sense of softness and fluidity and the silk a sense of polished durability.

It has been said both that her work has 'an absolute and organic violence' and that 'it does not excite or agitate but moves by its stillness and poignance'. There is nothing contradictory in these descriptions, or rather it is just this combination of elements and emotions that Chase-Riboud wants to evoke. Her work speaks both of the order and rigidity of the abstract and the chaos and fragility of the emotion and finally the absolute need for both.

'*Having been brought up and trained in the tradition of Western art evolved from Greco-Roman aesthetic, it was not until the beginning of the 60's that the authenticity, force, and historical validity of Eastern, Egyptian and African Art made itself vital to my artistic development. It was not until these influences were filtered through the grid of a certain modernism that I was exposed to at Yale University, as well as the explosion of Black consciousness of the late sixties and the impact of 'Pop' Art that my present style evolved. It is complex, baroque and in a sense esoteric in that there are many elements which are opposed to the overriding contemporary American influence in Art. Neither Eastern nor Western,*

'Bathers' 1972 15cm × 380cm × 432cm (6″ × 13′ × 14′) Aluminium and synthetic silk

neither European nor strictly American, neither 'Modern' nor classical, half pictorial and half architectural, it encompasses many disturbing and even aggressive elements. My work has often been described as 'beautiful' and 'highly finished', therefore 'classical' and 'European'. Yet, one could point out that the reverence for craftsmanship is even more an African and Far Eastern quality. Furthermore the deliberate choice of 'classic' materials is in a way a revolutionary approach to an aesthetic problem which is basically contemporary and intellectual: the combination of hard and soft materials. Not only is it a principal preoccupation of contemporary American art, but it lends itself to the idea of 'Anti-Art' extremely well. I, on the contrary, have chosen this idea (which for me, comes basically from the African dancing mask) to interpret in highly sculptural rather than intellectual terms (for example, a slab of glass and a rope). This is a deliberate choice based on love of craftsmanship as well as a revolt against 'Minimal Art'. I consider my expression 'Maximal Art'. More is not always better but less is not necessarily more profound nor more avant-garde.

The use of cord and rope skirts released me from the tyranny of the base and the armature and was an absolute revolution for me. I could be completely abstract in the plastic as well as the intellectual sense as the evocation of the human form as well as the architectural base were eliminated, liberating me to concentrate on the inner life of the abstract forms as poetry and magic, separate from both naturalistic and environmental reverberations. This leads to a richer, more complex surface,

complemented by the use of the lost-wax process in bronze, which is the most sensitive and versatile way of working metal. Intricate undercuts, carving and modelling are possible on a large scale as in no other process. I have pushed this process to the very limits of technique, and my surfaces are intricate and highly sensual on an architectural scale. This too is part of the combination of opposites that underlies all my work: hard and soft, dark and light, jewel-like and architectural, plastic or sensual and intellectual, rigid and yielding, improvision and control, weight bearing and weightlessness.

The silk and wool are worked not as a weaving material but as one would work clay, in mass and volume rather than weave and texture. This too is paradoxical in that the mass and heroic volume of the silk, a soft or feminine material, sometimes overwhelms the strength of the bronze, which in contrast is worked delicately and intricately. In one way, the silk is sculpted and the bronze woven . . . the overall impression is one of extreme tension and opposites pushed to the nth degree. This extreme tension and paradoxical inversion give what is on the surface a 'beautiful' object its underlying violence and disturbing quality. This 'dark underside' to beauty is the basis of my work.

The contradictions of my own racial and artistic heritage come to play in sculpture that I hope is a total as well as timeless expression of identity.'
Barbara Chase-Riboud, *Spectia*, August 29 1975.

Detailed biography on page 153.

'The Cape' 1973 2.5m × 1.5m × 1.5m (8′4″ × 5′ × 5′) Multi-coloured bronze, hemp and copper wire over steel armature

Left: 'Black Column' 3m × 56cm × 56cm (10′ × 1′10″ × 1′10″) Black-bronze and synthetic-silk-covered cords

'Monument to Malcolm X' 1970 2m × 1.5m × 20cm (7′ × 5′ × 8″) Polished bronze and synthetic silk
Right: 'Zanzibar' 1972 285cm × 85cm × 25cm (9′6″ × 2′10″ × 10″) Polished bronze and synthetic silk

Peter Collingwood

Peter Collingwood was born in 1922 in London. He studied medicine at St Mary's Hospital, qualifying in 1946, and then spent two years in the Army and a year with the Red Cross as a doctor.

However, early on in his professional medical career he had been much impressed by Eric Gill's words '. . . the thing you like doing should be your work' and because of this he decided to leave medicine and become, in due course, a weaver.

To this end, in 1950 he entered the studio of that pioneer spinner, dyer and handweaver Ethel Mairet at Ditchling in Sussex. After studying with her he moved to the studio of Barbara Sawyer in order to learn how to weave rugs and finally to the establishment of that other great pioneer weaver, but this time in the field of industrial textiles, Alistair Morton, at Carlisle. Morton's 'Edinburgh Weaver' range of furnishing fabrics were both a revelation and a revolution in the post-war Britain of the 1950's, bringing artistry to the product of the power loom—for so long lacking.

In 1952 Peter Collingwood set up his own rug-weaving studio in London and had his first one-man exhibition at Heals of Tottenham Court Road, a firm then, as now, in the forefront of interior design in its widest sense.

In 1958 he was invited to occupy a studio in Digwell House Arts Centre at Welwyn, where architects soon became aware of his textiles. By now his work was featured at the Design Centre in Haymarket and he was chosen to design a wall-hanging for the Council of Industrial Design which was presented to the Chairman, Sir Gordon Russell, when he retired.

The last change, geographically, came when Peter Collingwood and his family moved to their present home, the Old School at Nayland near Colchester in Essex. The flat, open landscape is, according to Peter, 'misty and unhealthy' but the Victorian school buildings provide a superb studio space. There are five looms, all of which Peter Collingwood has adapted in a most inventive manner to his own particular purposes.

He works in personally conceived techniques, a technique generally being the springboard for creative effort. The 'corduroy' weave for pile rugs, the 'shaft-switching' technique for flat rugs and 'macro-gauze' technique for airy, precise, orderly, geometric wall-hangings in which one sees unencumbered the beauty of the linear quality of fine thread. Lately he uses also the 'Sprang' technique in all its variations, from the airy to the monumental.

Peter Collingwood spends the major portion of his time weaving at his studio, with writing coming a close second. His 'Techniques of Rug Weaving', Faber and Faber, 1968, and 'Sprang', Faber & Faber, 1974, are both definitive works on the subjects. A third book on tablet weaving is to come. He does a certain amount of teaching and lecturing, much of it in the USA.

He has participated in innumerable exhibitions all over the world but recognition could be said to have really arrived with the Collingwood/Coper Exhibition at the Victoria & Albert Museum in 1969, at a time when it was still rare for big galleries and museums to feature anyone but painters and sculptors.

Peter Collingwood is a man of quiet, practical common sense who loves to weave. He is also that rare person who can combine true artistry with sound business sense. He has evolved his own particular techniques, which give him considerable freedom of design and allow him to produce his work at speed. This keeps it within a reasonable price range, thus allowing the maximum number of people to enjoy his vision at a personal level.

In 1974 Peter Collingwood was awarded the Order of the British Empire, for his work as a weaver.

'I like weaving; I am happy if others like my work sufficiently to buy it, so that I can continue weaving.'
Peter Collingwood, 1975

Detailed biography on page 153.

 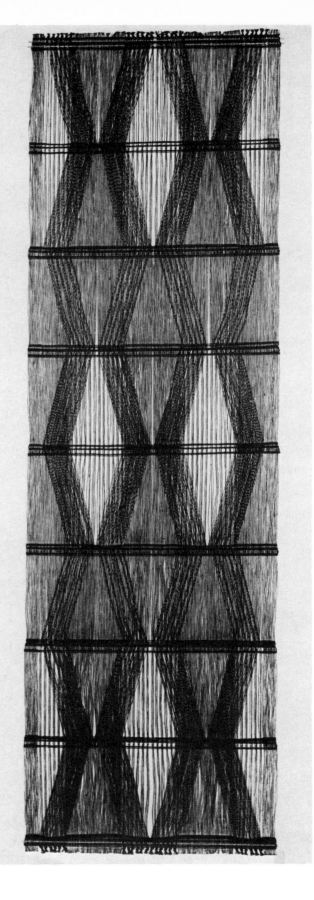

Above: 'Macrogauze No 86' 217cm × 82.5cm (87″ × 33″)
Bleached and unbleached linen, stainless steel rod

Left: 'Macrogauze No 46' 162cm × 50cm (65″ × 20″)
Black linen, stainless steel rod

Opposite left: 'Macrogauze No 31' 150cm × 45cm
(60″ × 18″) Black linen, stainless steel rod

Opposite far left: 'Macrogauze No 30' 219cm × 80cm
(88″ × 32″) Black linen, stainless steel rod

'Macrogauze No 56' 217cm × 93cm (87″ × 37″) Black linen, stainless steel rod

Left: 'Three-Dimensional Macrogauze No 5' Natural linen, stainless steel rod

Far left: 'Anglefell No 8' (detail) Bleached and unbleached linen

Daniel Graffin

Daniel Graffin is French; he was born in Paris in 1938 and now works there. After studying painting with L'hote and Aujame he received his Diplôme des Métiers d'Art in 1960. After that he served a period of time in the Army. Free of the Army, he learned Arabic and travelled to Egypt, where he remained for a year. While there he began to weave and to study natural dyeing in the workshop of the Egyptian architect, Wissa Wassef, with whom he developed a close rapport.

On his return to France he began work in the south, trying to give substance to his ideas via the medium of tapestry. He found little or no sympathetic dialogue amongst those functioning in tapestry in the traditional sense, for him 'tapestry existed and yet did not exist'; he felt very differently about his own research and wanted to go far beyond tapestry as such.

In 1973 he moved to a large, high studio in Paris. He works without a loom, tensioning framing structure-threads from floor to ceiling up to seven or eight metres high. Using this as a base structure, he then inserts the heavy-duty warp and the massive (often stuffed fabric tubes) wefts, manipulating them all by hand. He creates the exact line and curve of the edge of each section by stretching the strong guide lines at pre-defined angles so as to anchor the warp and weft, thus realising four-sided, totally finished selvedges. Both front and back of the pieces are worked vertically in space. In his monumental, soaring shapes one sees the total subservience of technique to concept. Indigo is the colour he most frequently employs. His newest work for the American Telegraph and Telephone Company juxtaposes deep blue leather with indigo cotton over a 30 square metre surface, stretched at great tension and anchored with turn-buckles into concrete. He says, 'the texture has now become the text'.

This is an artist who, having finally found his true medium and technique, now enjoys a total involvement with his work. His enormous woven statements, 'Situation Triangulaire' and 'Indigo Quadrangulaire', have been shown in the past two Biennales of Lausanne. Both works have a mystical, if not magical, quality and awe with their sense of soaring isolation. It would seem he has indeed used tapestry as a vehicle beyond which to move far.

'I do not portray faces, shapes. Rather I seek to imprison forces. I find accomplices in the dwellings of the spiders.
Ask a spider when she is preparing her snare if she can already see the fly coming: I weave because I lack a picture,

'Situation Quadrangulaire' 4m × 6m × 4.5m (13′ × 20′ × 15″) 1975 Musée des Arts Décoratifs, Paris

and this web, which is the weaving, seems to me sufficient snare.

You will, no doubt, ask, why tapestry?

Yes why tapestry, rather than painting or sculpture?

Painting, the picture is too obvious . . . it hides "the other"— which lies beyond it. They call my work a veil: I do not weave a veil, rather I unweave an opaque veil. The whole movement is reversed— I do not seek to fill space, but rather to empty it in order to create this very lack, this something belonging to space, which is registered in the negative of space.

The picture . . .

Up till a few years back, I wrestled with presentation, which was inseparable from textile support . . . now there is no more such support, because there is no more separation, the pretext is dead, buried, aspirated by texture—it has become the actual text.

The tension . . .

A sail is no use in dead calm weather, it simply exists there: then comes the wind and fills the sail, this has become a wind snare, the needlework of drawsheets (strips of canvas which make up the sail) are formed to enclose maximum pressures

which the wind will exercise at one single point, which is called the velic (woven) point.

That's how I work, trying to establish an initial triangulation on which will exercise the flexions of the entirety of the forces, which tend to lead the tapestry towards its central point.

The analogy stops there, because, in my world there is no wind, my sails would be those of the underwater sailor, imprisoned, or of an ice barrier, where every colour is ultimately lost.

Indigo . . .

Yet another fascination, obtained by the mineralisation of putrefied plant. The colouring processes are mechanical ones, involving the capturing of particles of indigo in the actual fibre . . . still the spider and fly situation . . .

Tapestry is therefore the subversion of the picture, of space and of colour.'

Daniel Graffin 1975

Detailed biography on page 154.

Top left and right, and above: **Details from 'Indigo 234'**   *Above:* **'Nilat Tawilat'** (detail)

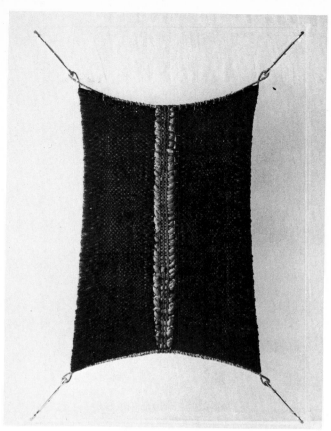

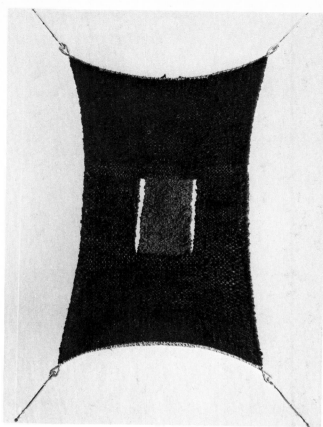

'Nilat Tawilat' 1975 120cm × 80cm (4′ × 2′8″)

'Firqan' 1975 120cm × 80cm (4′ × −′8″)

'Nilat Tawilat' (detail)

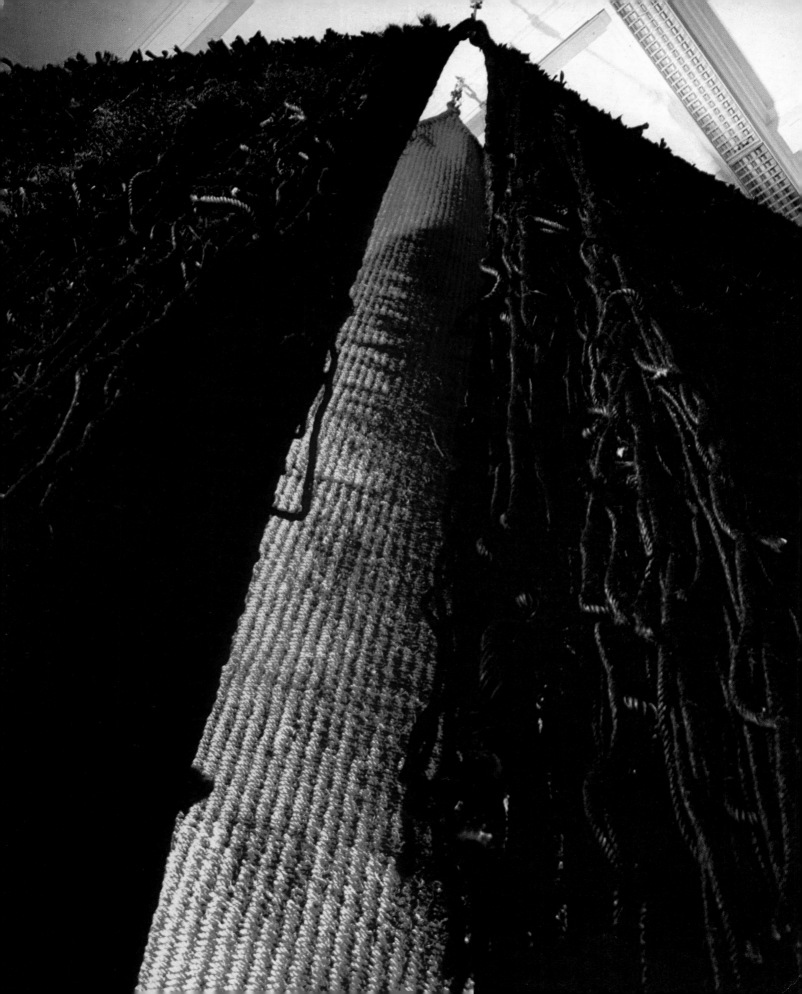

'Situation Triangulaire' 1973 *Left:* **Detail**

Josep Grau-Garriga

Josep Grau-Garriga was born in 1929 in Sant Cugat del Valles, Barcelona, Spain. He is an artist, spiritually rooted in his homeland, whose message is concern for, involvement with and love of man. This powerful and expressive message comes through with equal force whether he is working in paint, inks, fabrics, fibres or stained glass.

Between 1943 and 1947 he studied graphics and interior design at the Escuela d'Arts i Officis in Barcelona and between 1947 and 1951 studied painting at the Escuela' Superior de Bellas Artes de Barcelona, where he later became drawing instructor. He began to exhibit his paintings and by 1954 was working on large murals for various cities and churches in Catalonia.

In 1957 he produced his first cartoons for tapestries and in the following year made a study trip through Europe working for some time in the atelier of Jean Lurçat. Returning to Barcelona, he became the director of the Escuela' Catalana de Tapis, where he directed the translation into tapestry of his own work as well as that of artists like Picasso and Miro.

There followed years of steady artistic progress in the fields of painting, graphics, tapestry and, by 1963, stained glass. His paintings were often of mixed media and his tapestries were growing more and more textural and three-dimensional.

In 1967 his work was exhibited for the first time in the States and again in 1968. In 1969 he was invited by the International Institute, New York, to live in New York and to travel to visit centres of art in the States, Canada and Mexico. This experience had the effect of finally freeing his work totally from any lingering remnants of traditional attitudes to technique which may, however distantly, have still been inhibiting him. From then on both his painting and his 'tapestries' shook free, paintings encompassing collage and assemblage, and tapestries becoming three-dimensional, free-standing or free-hanging, sculptural forms of tremendous force and power.

Grau-Garriga believes that 'textile fibres and textures offer proper characteristics in themselves; materials, like words, can provide great eloquence . . . too often people are interested in language problems only for language rather than for content'. Of the loom as tool he says, 'It is a challenge to the imagination, without the framework of the loom we would soon fall into artifice, facility, trickery . . .'. His enormous pieces are produced in the atelier under his constant supervision, although since 1970 he has found it necessary to take a much more absolute and total involvement in their actual creation. His works seem inextricable from the people, colour, landscape and architecture of his native Catalonia. One feels that his concept of his works goes beyond their measurable limits and into their settings, like the sculpture of Henry Moore which sits so timelessly in vast landscape. His output of work is prodigious and the number of exhibitions in which it has been seen, either one-man or collective, are legion. It is in museums, galleries and collections all over Europe and the States but the area in which he lives, and particularly the churches, is the richest testament to his vigour and artistry.

'In my work, I make use of the object (specially in painting) that has personal connotations. It seems to me more valid and authentic to use simple forms than beautiful ones. I am much more interested with reality itself than in representation. In tapestry I use materials that are tied to my memories and the image of my land. I try to reaffirm their value so that they speak for themselves, I only want to make evident what is already there. I am very much in love with life and it is maybe because of that I am frequently touched by its sarcastic drama.

To me the work of art should be the author's own reflection. After it achieves liberty, it cannot avoid to denounce injustice, to introduce new forms, to meet and to express itself as an absolute lover of beauty in every sense.

I believe that the most important thing that I can say about my work is that it is more than an attempt to communicate my sensations to other people. These intimate sensations are strengthened and motivated by the exterior world for which I feel a total love. Every factor of life affects me, especially when there is a problem. By natural inclination, I take sides with the

'Monument a l'Esperantça' 1974 4.5m × 3m × 2m (15′ × 10′ × 7′)

persecuted minorities and for the revindications that I believe contest, I cannot stay indifferent in front of this and therefore take a partisan position.

From all that, we learn that in my work the most important element is what I try to say than the way I say it. I believe that the content in the work of art is what communicates the

artist's feelings to people. I am interested in the problem of forms, for they are to me useful to express myself in my own way, but I see very clearly the aesthetic problems.'
Josep Grau-Garriga, Barcelona, 1975

Detailed biography on page 154.

'El Roie es Vida' 1975

'Venus Fosca' 1975
Right: 'Parella' 1974 2.3m × 1.5m (7′8″ × 5′)

'Naixemont d'un Rei' 1973

Left : 'Soca de Guernica' 1973 2.35m × 1m × 90cm
(8′ × 3′4″ × 3′)

Right : 'De Soca i Arren' 1972 (detail)

Françoise Grossen

Françoise Grossen is Swiss and was born in Neuchatel in 1943. She is therefore among the younger practising artists. She now lives in New York.

In 1963 and 1964 she studied in the School of Architecture of Lausanne University. Extended travel in Africa at this point was to be a very strong influence and more travel there ensued in 1965 and 1967. She entered the Department of Textile Design at Basel School of Arts and Crafts, where she obtained her degree in 1967. A very important thing then happened, she exhibited in a show in Zurich with Sheila Hicks, Lenore Tawney and Claire Zeisler and this encounter crystallised her desire to study and work in the States. She moved to California to work under Professor Bernard Kester at the University of California in Los Angeles, where she found a very sympathetic ambience, and obtained her Masters Degree in Textiles in 1969.

Her first post was that of designer in the Jack Lenor Larsen studio in New York, where she received enormous encouragement. Two pieces of her work were included on the 'Wall Hangings' exhibition at the New York Museum of Modern Art. In 1971 she became textile instructor at the New School, New York, and at the Art School of the Brooklyn Museum, New York, Her work was now being bought extensively for public and private collections and she began to execute architect-commissioned works.

In 1973 she began to concentrate almost entirely on her own work, participating now and then in summer schools and workshops in various parts of the USA. Her work has been shown consistently at Lausanne in the Biennales of 1969, 1971, 1973 and 1975, and is illustrated in major works on textile artists.

Her works are organic in concept. Her materials are massive cords and ropes which stream groundwards, come together, separate and form areas of massive, three-dimensional curving fabric. The nature of her materials pre-determines, to some extent, the colour of her work which has been either natural or earth colours, but is now changing slightly. Her techniques are mainly knotting and braiding.

The loft studio in which she works is situated at the very top of a warehouse in Greenwich Village, New York. Being high up, it is full of light, which is reflected in the polished wooden floor. The massive curved arches of the basic structure of the building can be seen in the brickwork of the walls. Here the artist's rope objects tower and hang between floor and ceiling and snake over the floor, creating a distinctly forest-like ambience.

'My work is my statement.'
Françoise Grossen, New York, 1975

Detailed biography on page 155.

'Cinq Rivières' (detail)

'Cinq Rivières' 1974 2.2m × 2.4m (7′5″ × 8′ × 2′) Sisal braiding

'Inchworm' 1973 (detail) 6m × 4.5m × 7.5m (20′ × 15′ × 25′) Amber rubber hose

'Untitled' 1974 3m × 1.5m × 75cms (10′ × 5′ × 2′6″) Manila rope

'Five White Elements' 1971 3.3m × 1.5m (11′ × 5′) Macramé knotting in white cotton piping cord
Left: 'Embarcadero' 1973 (detail) Sisal and metal. Regency Hyatt House, San Francisco

Ted Hallman

Ted Hallman was born in Bucks County, Pennsylvania in 1933 and his adult life seems to be shared between this, his home ground, and California.

He combines many activities, being both an innovative and uninhibited constructor in fibre and thread and also a weaver who delights in the complexities of traditionally based fabric constructions. He is an artist producing textile objects, a designer for the textile industry, a consultant and juror and, not least, an enthusiastic teacher. Of his teaching he says he is 'interested in helping students to find their own resources for expression from their own lives and inner sources and to work from their own creative centres'. His approach to 'nurturing creative expression' has grown out of an understanding of Jungian psychology; study of body movement and dance; and a body therapy called 'structural integration'.

He first studied at Tyler School of Fine Arts, Temple University, Philadelphia, obtaining his B.F.A. and his B.Sc. in Education in 1956, then to Cranbrook Academy of Arts, Michigan, to gain his M.F.A.s in Painting and in Textile Design in 1958.

For the next five years he wove, created forms in thread, designed for the textile industry and for interior designers and architects, taught in many parts of the United States, travelled, doing a period of study in Austria, won several major prizes and scholarships and had his work exhibited. It was at this point in his progress, as an artist, that he was producing the transparent 'screens' which use threads like a pen-line, and later the tree series and the three-dimensional 'hammock'.

In 1963 he became Head of the Textile Department at Moore College of Art, Philadelphia, where he remained for five years, during which time he was textile consultant to Jamaica for the U.N. In 1970 he returned to full-time study, working for his PhD in Education at the University of California at Berkeley, when his dissertation was 'The Nurturance of Creative Expression in the Adult'. During his time at Berkeley he taught at several universities in California and he is now Professor of Textiles at San José State College, California.

'The forms which I use in fibre pieces have evolved from their sense of construction and structure. Initially, I was interested in building a floor loom and when that was completed, I learned to weave. This led me into the structures of fabrics to which there seems to be no end. For a long time I worked on placing dyed and textured plexiglass (perspex) forms structurally into open weave fabrics. The forms which evolved were an outgrowth of the shapes the yarns made when woven around the integrated materials. These pieces were used as room dividers and window treatments and, along with other fabrics, were often made on commission basis for architects and interior designers to use in public buildings.

Double weave has always been a great love and challenge. Out of double weave came checkerboard fabrics and seamless garments. Then I became interested in three-dimensional structures, sometimes using other techniques than weaving, like knitting, and later environments made of yarns. Along with this work smaller pieces have been developed which are stretch woven on small frames, also on-going series of hammocks and some woven designs for industrial production.

I prefer to begin a work with a vision of the end product. I make many drawings—before, during and sometimes even after the piece is completed. I like to let the vision change as the developing work makes its demands. This keeps the process lively for me. Although I have designed several printed pieces, I prefer to accentuate the structural aspects of my work and what occurs as design and decoration are outgrowths from this foundation.

I find teaching quite stimulating. It's fun to invent ways to play with fabric in space and to move with yardages. Rituals of sound, light, fabric, movement, etc are wonderful to stage for people who love fabrics and, likewise, the exploration of design in architectural settings or developing garments by studying body movement in a workshop situation. But, even more, I enjoy teaching the technology of fabric construction and pattern. The challenge is to make the presentation so simple, clear and direct that it can be understood easily. It delights me that the area of textiles has such a broad range of possible expressions.'

Ted Hallman, California, May 1975.

Biographical details on page 155.

'Centering Environment' 1969 Woven cube; acrylic fibres on steel frame

'Alby's Tree' 3.6m (12′) high. Interlaced cotton

Right: Detail of acrylics woven into fabric.
Smithsonian Collection.

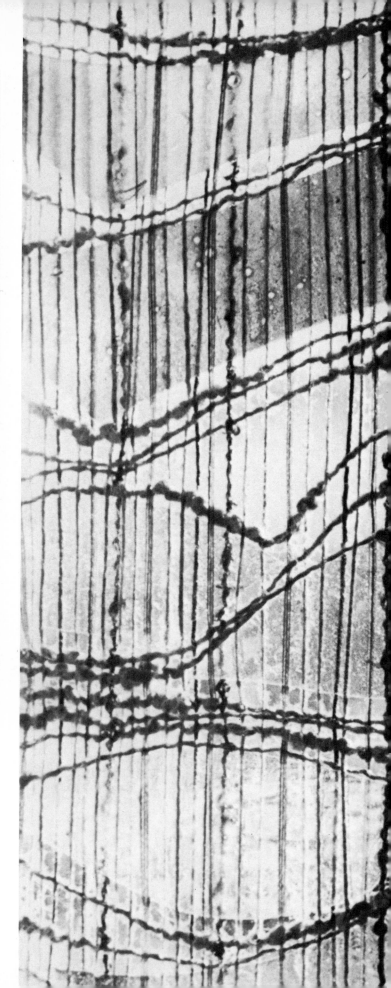

'Hammock' Johnson Collection
Right : 'Tree Form' 3.9m × 1.5m (13′ × 5′) Cotton

Far right : 'Tree Form' (detail)

Sheila Hicks

Sheila Hicks is American by birth and lives with her family in Paris. A spirit of perseverance in her pioneer grandparents, plus a mixed cultural ancestry, are two important factors in her background.

Involvement with cloth and thread was a practical part of her youth. Her early skills and inclinations were both physical and intellectual, but on entering Syracuse University, New York, in 1952 she elected to take a fine arts course and she drew, painted and studied printmaking. After two years, she transferred to Yale University, New Haven, to study painting with Josef Albers. She became fascinated with pre-Inca textiles, wrote a paper on them and started weaving herself. At about this time, she met Lenore Tawney, with whom she was later to exhibit together with Claire Zeisler, and realise the first modern weaving shows in the United States and Europe (The Museum of Contemporary Crafts, New York, 1963, and the Kunstgewerbemuseum, Zurich, 1964). Her 'miniatures' became known, and she enlarged the format of her exploration. Photography began to be an important area of research for her and she recorded all that interested her as she travelled through South America (on a Fulbright

Scholarship) and Europe (Fribourg grant). In Mexico in 1961 she held her first one-woman weaving show at the Souza Gallery.

At this period she was using the Ikat technique, that is, the tight, spot-wrapping of long, laid out warp, extensively. The frequent contact with the Mexican craftsmen in the Tenancingo area was to influence her greatly.

Wrapping is evident in the first of her 'Prayer Rug' series created in West Germany. The hand-technique compliments the mechanical tufting in the large, wool, rugs incorporating masses of fringe.

It was one of these prayer rugs, installed on a granite wall of the C.B.S. Building in New York, which began her very direct involvement with architecture. The architects of the Ford Foundation in New York required that thread be used not as ornament but as a construction material; this coincided with her approach to her materials.

Two entire walls were constructed by embroidering honey-coloured silk 'Medallions' over the forty-four and thirty-two square metre surfaces. Next, she designed and made three complete rooms as fibre environments for Georg Jensen's Centre for Advanced Design in New York: a linen, forested, tasselled room called 'Lion's Lair', a silk floss, pale green, stitched 'Ritual Chamber', and tiny mohair 'bricks' sewn on all four walls, floor to ceiling, for 'Sweater Room'.

Simultaneously, while producing these two innovative

architectural projects, Sheila Hicks was also engaged in designing, in a more practical manner, with weavers of a large hand-weaving workshop in India. This experience resulted not only in a superb range of beautiful fabrics, but also inspired a further series of wall-hangings. In the past eight years she has produced three separate collections of hand-woven cottons and silks with this group. Daniel Graffin, the French tapestry artist, collaborated with her on the ONAM collection. They have also exhibited together in Nantes and New Zealand and, most recently, in the mammoth tapestry exhibition at the Musée des Arts Decoratifs, Paris, May 1975.

Immediately after India, she returned to South America to organise a community of shepherds to support themselves by weaving. Again the results, in spite of political and economical setbacks, were successful. Since 1970 she has been engaged in producing original wall-rugs with craftsmen in Morocco: many of these were exhibited in Rabat, Tunis, Abdijan and Dakar (1970–75).

Her work is in innumerable buildings and museums throughout the world. Her silk tapestries are installed in the passenger cabins of nineteen Air France Jumbo Jets. Work-in-progress reveals further versatility in both design and construction (a bank lobby in Little Rock, Gallería in New York, Fiat Tower in Paris, Camino Real and IBM in Mexico). In 1974 she was awarded a gold medal by the American Institute of Architects and the Stedelijk Museum, Amsterdam gave a retrospective of her work in 1974. She underlines the beauty of threads when used in the mass as no other artist does, with both a reverence and an exuberance, so that one is aware of nothing but the sheer magnificence of the material and her handling of it. The resulting works are poems of thread. In the sensuousness and intelligence of her statements, she is a true artist with astounding strength, force and energy. If this were not enough, when she is in a teaching situation, her personality is as engaging and as all-encompassing as her work and she opens herself up completely to the job of communicating at a deep and meaningful level.

'Weaving is no more and no less than weaving. That means it can be everything for some and nothing for others. For me it is a rudimentary form of expression enabling the greatest access to my own dream world . . . .'
Sheila Hicks, Lausanne Biennale, 1975.

Detailed biography on page 155.

Top right: 'Malabar Harvest' 1972 4.5m × 2m (14′9″ × 6′7″) Synthetic and cotton thread mixed; woven and braided

Right: 'Vague Orange' 1973 3.8m × 1.8m (12′6″ × 5′11″) Linen and synthetic wrapped with cotton, composed of 80 modular elements

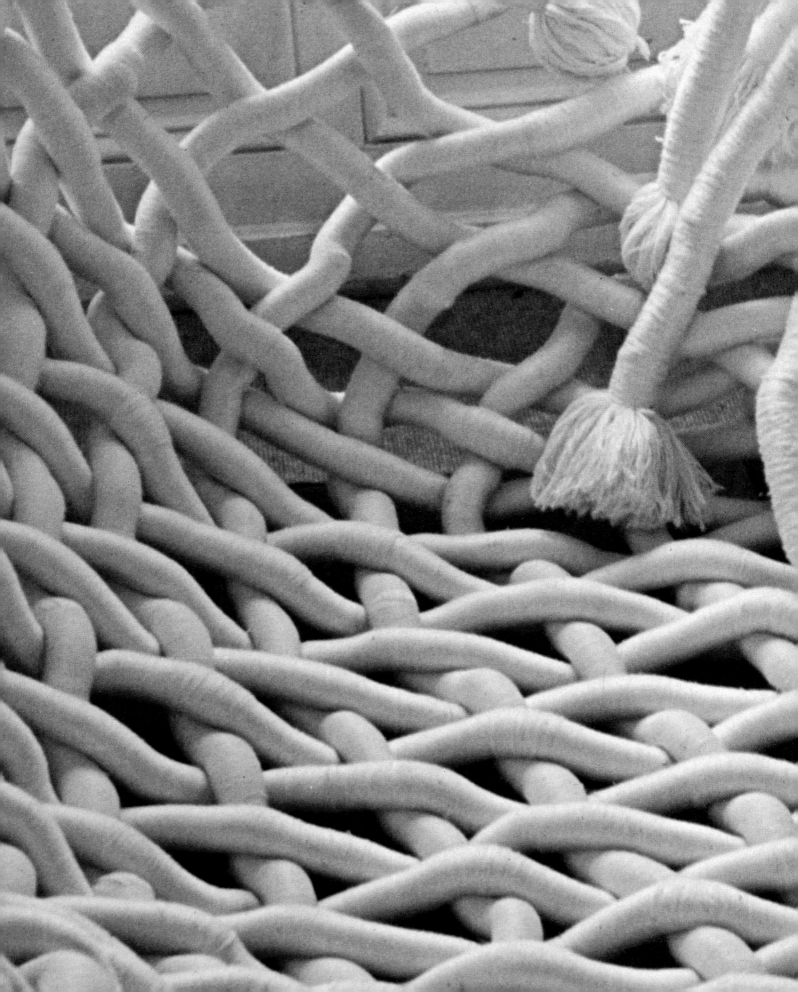

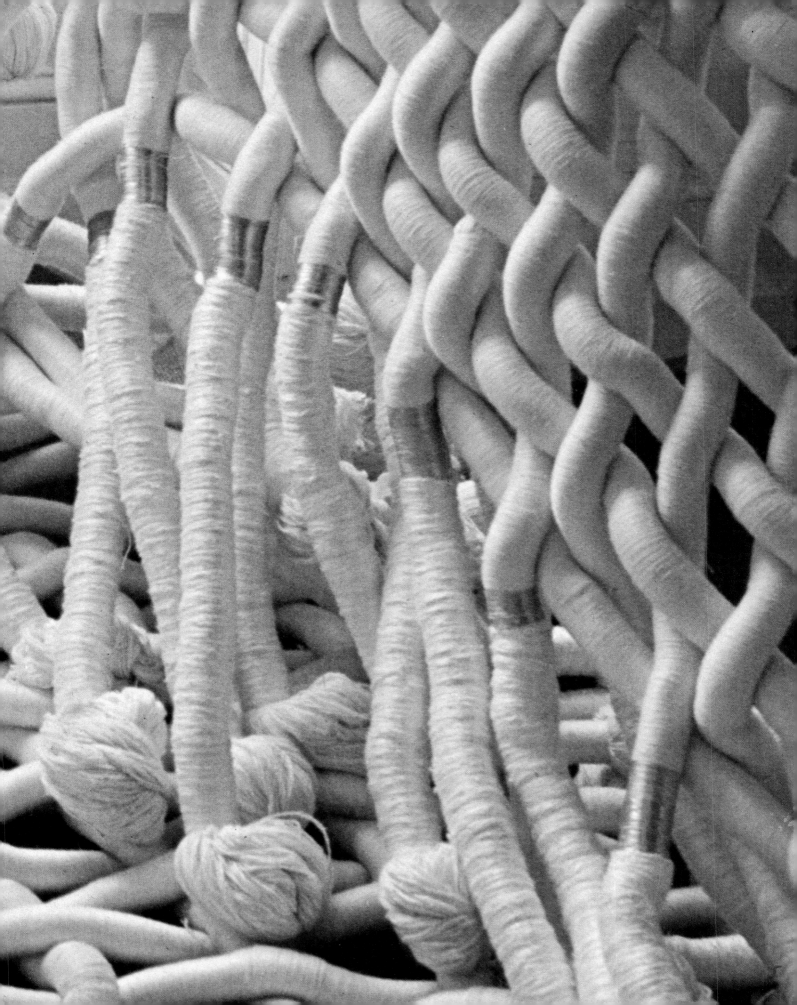

'Medallions' 1967 4m × 11m and 4m × 8m (13′1″ × 36′1″ and 13′1″ × 26′3″) Two panels, silk embroidered on seamless linen cloth. Installed at the Ford Foundation, New York.

Right: 'Ritual Chamber' (detail) 1968 2.8m × 4.8m (9′2″ × 15′9″) Silk floss embroidered on hand-woven silk textile, six panels. Installed at the Georg Jensen Centre for Advanced Design, New York

Far right: Textile bas-relief in linen and gold threads (detail)

Previous page: 'Macro Tissage' 1973 3.5m × 3.5m (11′ × 11′) Bleached linen wrapped around cotton and fibrane then woven. Exhibited Musée des Arts Decoratifs, Paris, 1975

'Lianes Nantaises' 1973 5m × 1.6m (16′5″ × 5′3″) Natural linen wrapped with silk, wool, synthetic raffia. Exhibited, Musée des Arts Decoratifs, Nantes

Right : 'Arc-en-Barrois' 6.1m × 5.49m × 5.49m (20′ × 18′ × 18′) A 'macro-tissage' built up *sur place* at the 7th Biennale of Tapestry, Lausanne; silk-bound modular elements, purple and brown.

Ritzi and Peter Jacobi

Ritzi and Peter Jacobi are both Roumanian by birth and now live in West Germany.

Ritzi was born in Bucharest in 1941, Peter in Ploesti in 1935. Both studied at the Institul de Arte Plastice in Bucharest though at different periods and in different subjects, Ritzi studying tapestry weaving techniques, painting and drawing there between 1960 and 1966, and Peter studying sculpture between 1954 and 1961.

Each worked at their own medium until a year after their marriage in 1966, when they began to merge ideas and techniques to produce works which now seem the product of one mind. They moved to Germany in 1970.

They have an atelier in Neubarental in the Black Forest, where they work together on the formulation of their ideas and the production of the final works. Their work now shows a total fusion of tapestry weaving, drawing and sculpture, sculptural and graphic forms being worked out in textile terms. In their most recent works the total object is three-dimensional with wound and bound growth springing forward from a tapestry base fabric of the utmost textile validity, soft yet firm, hanging not stretched, and using to the full the complex nuances possible from the tapestry technique to enhance the feeling of textile, the feeling of the three-dimensional and to create an insoluble link between base-weave and outgrowths.

Their work has changed and evolved during the nine years they have been working together. It seems to have become stronger, gentler, more lyrical, less aggressive and, most important of all, more total in its mastery of absorbing the onlooker into itself, stilling the mind with its strong, gentle totality of form and sombre yet lively use of natural fibres and colours.

Peter has since 1972 incorporated teaching into his activities, while Ritzi takes a major part in the actual production, with the aid of some assistants. But, however it is organised, the astonishing factor is firstly the quiet power, enormous presence and vivid imagery of the work and, secondly, the complete fusion of two minds to produce one perfect art form.

Detailed biography on page 156.

'Transylvania I' 1973 5m × 4m × 1.5m (16′5″ × 13′2″ × 4′11″) Tapestry with drawing; goathair, rice paper

'Transylvania II' 1974 3m × 6m × 1m (9′10″ × 19′8″ × 3′4″) Tapestry, horsehair and goathair. Collection Kunsthalle Mannheim.

'Exotica IV' 1975 2.6 × 1.9m (8′7″ × 6′3″) Tapestry with goathair and natural wool. *Right*: Detail

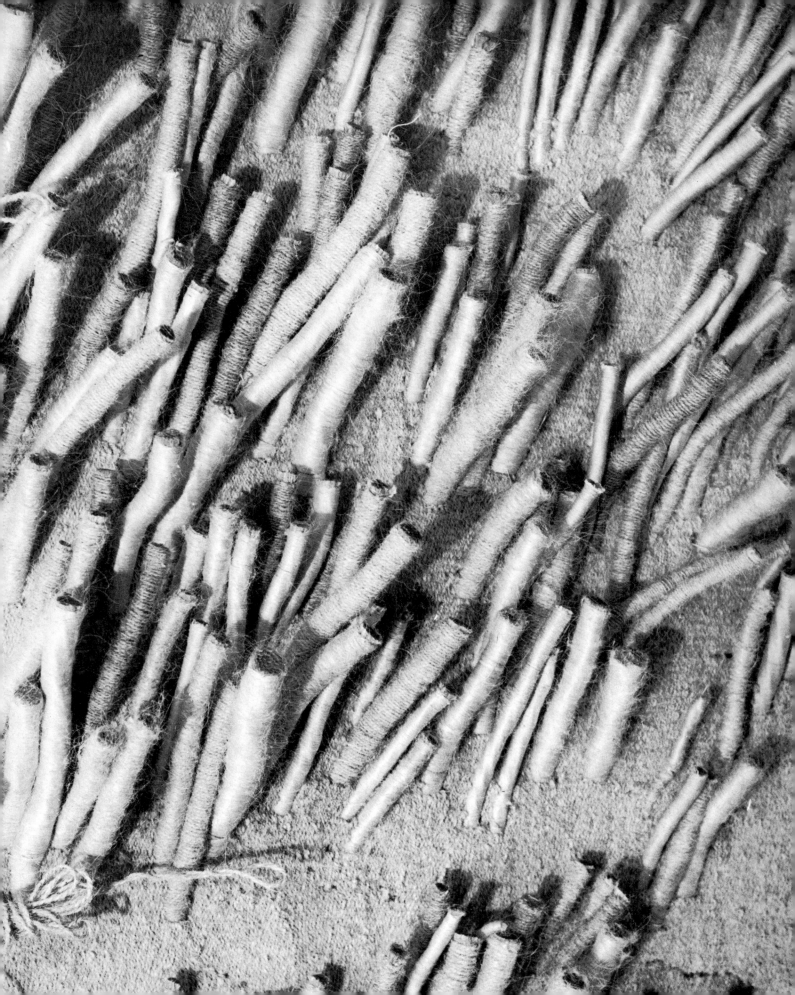

'Environment Variable II' 1970 Weaving and winding; wool

'Exotica III' 1975 2.5m × 6′7″) Tapestry with cables, goathair, horsehair, sisal and cotton

Gerhardt Knodel

Gerhardt Knodel was born in Milwaukee, Wisconsin, in 1940.

From 1957 to 1959 he studied at Los Angeles City College and from 1959 to 1962 worked for his Bachelor of Arts Degree in Textiles at the University of California, Los Angeles, under Bernard Kester.

From 1962 to 1968 he taught art in various Los Angeles' city schools, from 1965 to 1970 in the adult division. During this time he was doing a great deal of study and research into contemporary and historic textiles in Europe and in the States, often for the purpose of understanding historic precedents for work with which he is currently involved.

From 1968 to 1970 he studied for his Master of Arts Degree in Textiles with Mary Jane Leland at California State College, Long Beach, lecturing in art at the College at the same time.

In 1970 he became head of the Fabric Design Department of Cranbrook Academy of Art, Bloomfield Hills, Michigan, the establishment which produces so many great creative textile artists.

His study of historic textiles continues, now mostly in India.

Since 1960 his work has been widely exhibited in the States and Canada. He is, however, not a very well-known artist in Europe, his work probably being seen for the first time at the 1975 7th International Biennale of Tapestry at Lausanne.

He is unique in the objects he produces. Although the work has, of necessity, changed over the years, probably growing more airy and less earth-bound, always there has been a preoccupation with the behaviour of fabric in space, an essential element being the action of the surrounding atmosphere upon it. This has sometimes taken shape in the form of vast tents and canopies.

Arten Luin says, of work shown at the Detroit Institute of Arts, 'he explores the relationships of man and fibre that go beyond familiar experience . . . he is concerned about that which is "sensed" by his audience and the heightened awareness which results from experiencing familiar materials in an unusual context. Movement is essential, not only in the kinetic experiences created by surrounding the viewer with the breathing cloth, but also in relief wall structures which reflect a frozen millesecond of time/experience. His works are full of adventure . . .'.

'Architecture is the setting for man's activities. The space which exists within the confines of walls, floor and ceiling, as found in most buildings created by man, becomes the stage for the activities of living.

Contrary to the variety and flexibility of activity that occur within the home environment, the physical enclosure for these activities, once established, remains characteristically constant regardless of the mood of happening within the walls.

If the home can be regarded as the theatre for the drama of living, it seems that the home environment should be flexible, pliable and easily movable. In contrast, American homes have traditionally incorporated fabric only as functional floor covering, window drapery and furniture upholstery, usually without concern for the inherent qualities of fabrics that might allow for greater variety and inventiveness in environmental application.

I visualize fabric structures as the means of inventively shaping and adjusting the rectangular modular volume which seems to have become the standard shape of living space for contemporary man.

If the economics of the architectural approach for designing spaces for human habitation imposes a commonness of spatial enclosure in the life of every man, perhaps it is for the individual, with his innate desire to function as an individual, to change this imposed space, creating something which is more flexible according to human need, indeed reflective of the flexible nature of man.

The qualities of fabric seem to suggest it as an ideal medium for developing a kind of visual and functional spatial flexibility.'
Gerhardt Knodel, 1972

Detailed biography on page 156.

Above: **Two views of 'Act 8' 1974 2.4m × 3m × 4.3m
(8′ × 10′ × 14′) Suspended movable enclosure/environment;
silk, printed, batiked, dyed; multi-coloured red, blue green**

Left: **'Parhelic Path' 1974 5.5m × 12m × 2.7m
(18′ × 40′ × 9′) Movable fabric plane; handwoven
mylar, rayon**

Previous page: **'Parhelic Path' (detail)**

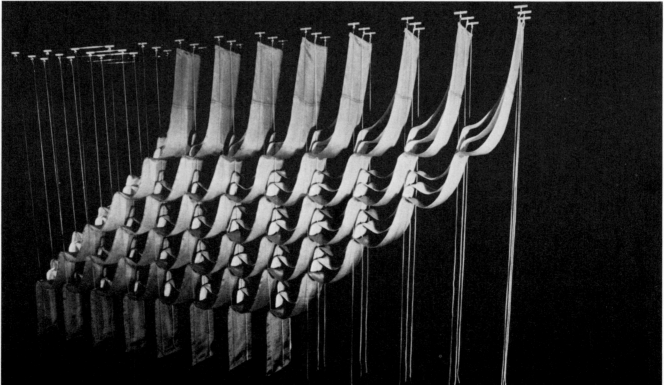

Top : **'Up and Away' 1974 Movable sculpture** *Right :* **'Up and Away' Alternative configuration**

Above: '**Flank Right**' **1974 Prototype for movable architectural wall**

Walter Nottingham

Walter Nottingham is American and was born in Great Falls, Montana, in 1930.

From 1956 he studied at St Cloud State College, Minnesota, there obtaining his Bachelor's and Master's Degrees in Textiles in 1958 and 1959.

In 1962 he was appointed associate professor in the Textile Department of the University of Wisconsin at River Falls where he has lived and worked, with gaps, ever since, finding himself much in tune with the landscape and general ambience of Wisconsin. Since his appointment he has studied further at Haystack School of Crafts in Maine and at Cranbrook Academy of Arts, Michigan, where he obtained his Master's Degree in Fine Art in 1968.

He has been visiting professor or artist in residence at many distinguished art schools and he presents workshops and gives lectures throughout the United States and also in Canada. His work has been exhibited in innumerable shows, possibly the most important being Objects USA 1969, the Lausanne Biennale of 1971, the Wall Hanging International Exhibition of 1968 at the New York Museum of Modern Art, and several other major exhibitions in New York. His work is illustrated in many books and publications.

From being basically a weaver, he has moved towards the use of crochet as a major technique. His work often being organic, enclosed shapes with lots of movement and life both physical and spiritual implied, the complex intestine-like crocheted forms anchoring falls of streaming yarns. Another technigue he is concerned with is twining (see 'Rope Shrine').

He is a very private person in his attitudes to his work but generous in spirit to his friends, students and those who share his preoccupations. He is unimpressed by the public adulation which artists can receive, remaining apart and aloof from this aspect of life and concerning himself with the work alone.

He lives with his family in a timber and glass house set deep in woodlands and the house and its setting seem to merge. His studio is apart from but attached to the house and one senses that he and his family and his natural retreat-like ambience are one.

'Each work is my attempt to articulate through fibres spiritual, emotional and aesthetic impulses. Fibre construction and fibre manipulation, both on and off the loom, is the major form (medium) into and through which I attempt to translate, discover, intensify and respond to the mystical aspects of my life.

The atmosphere or mystic aura is the main concern of my work. Technical means are, for me, always secondary. The

form and technique, I feel, must be 'one' developed from the foundation of a search for content—a groping for expressive, symbolic images within the life-cycle of a work. The work makes itself through my hands.

The search for the forms of things unknown—not trying to make the visible seen but the unseen visible, a probing of the mystical content within my life and the medium of fibres is my involvement as a weaver.

I believe that fibres have within its aura a pent-up energy, an intense life of their own. I am attempting to explore this unreal reality, this often unseen but felt content of fibres. To try and capture and make visible those elusive qualities of the extra-sensory aspect present within the world around and within me.'
Walter Nottingham, 1975

Detailed biography on page 157.

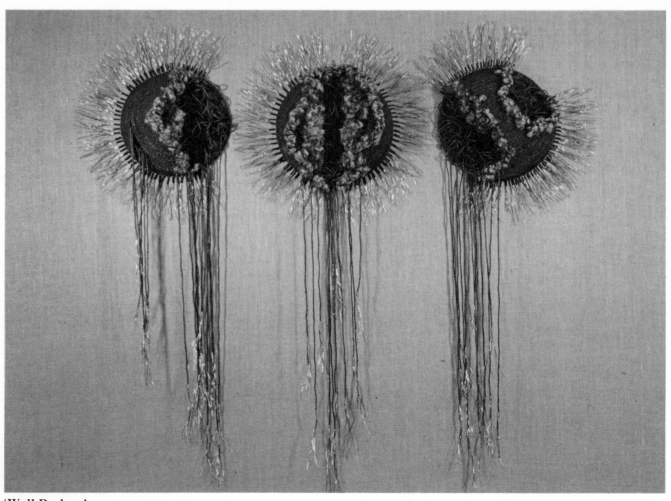

'Wall Baskets'

Right : **'Celibacy' 2.74m × 91.5cm × 61cm (9′ × 3′ × 2′)
Crocheted wool**

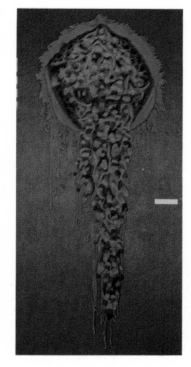

'Rope Shrine' (detail, see previous page)

Far right : **'Rope Shrine' 2.13m × 1.83m × 61cm
(7′ × 6′ × 2′) Coiling and twining; sisal, linen, jute,
manila**

Above : '**Crocheted Form**'
Right : '**Pillar**' **Weaving and winding**

Left : '**Neskowin**' **In two parts: Part 1**
274cm × 91.5cm × 61cm (9′ × 3′ × 2′) Woven and
crocheted horse and camel hair. Part 2:
91.5cm × 91.5cm × 61cm (3′ × 3′ × 2′) Crocheted and
wrapped horse and camel hair

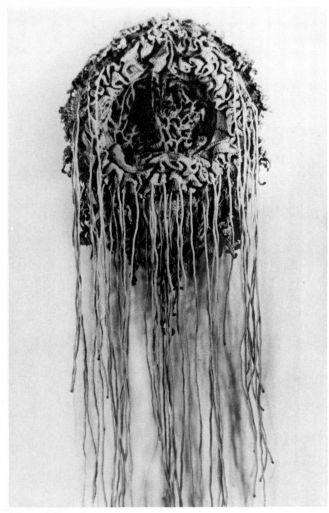

'Fuses' Crochet

'Wall Pillow' Crochet

'Soul Touch' 2.9m × 1.5m × 6m (9½′ × 5′ × 2′) Wool,
rayon, dacron; multiple-layer weaving and knotting

Wojciech Sadley

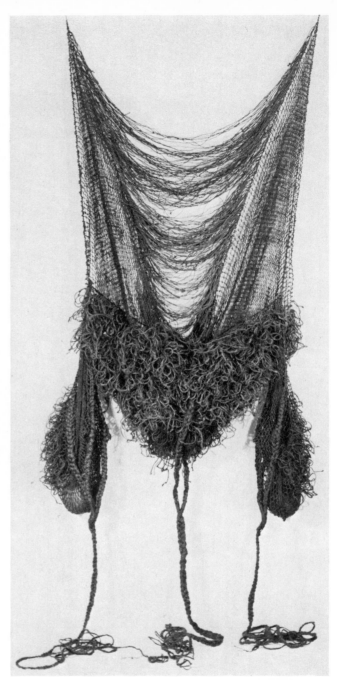

'He II' 1971 3.5m × 1.5m (12′ × 5′) **Netting, braiding and pile**

Wojciech Sadley is Polish and was born in Lublin in 1932.

From 1949 to 1959 he studied at the Academia Sztuk Pieknych (Academy of Fine Arts) in Warsaw in the Departments of Painting and Interior Architecture, gaining his Diploma in Interior Architecture in 1954 and in Painting in 1959. He studied also at the Music Conservatory. Thus we have a painter/musician/interior designer.

From 1959 to 1967 he was engaged on scientific and research work in the Department of Light and Colour of the Institut Wzornictwa Przemyslowego (Institute of Industrial Design) in Warsaw, thus adding a further dimension to his skill and experience. During this time he was steadily pursuing his own artistic preoccupations in his Warsaw studio, producing the immense, dark, brooding, pendulous works which characterise him. 'Mixed media' is an oft-used term when describing contemporary art; to Sadley's work it really applies as his works may be sprayed, painted or printed fabric, hung, pulled and formed into shapes or mixed with streaming threads, huge areas of netting and shapes of wood or metal or like materials.

In 1967 he was appointed Assistant Professor in the Department of Painting at the Academy of Fine Arts with special responsibility for the pursuance of experimental textile art. He is now head of the Faculty of Tapestry and a revered artist in his own country and known world-wide.

His work is in many museums and public buildings in Poland, Europe, America and Japan and he has received numerous art awards in Poland and elsewhere. From about 1962 his work has been exhibited internationally and he has the distinction of having been included in all six of the first Lausanne Biennales.

Detailed biography on page 157

'Tantos' 1973 2.5m × 1m (8′ × 3′2″)

Left : 'Trio II' 1973 (detail) 2.5m × 50cm ×(8′ × 1′9″) Netting, winding, braiding and pile

'Imar' 1967 3m × 2m (10′ × 6′9″) Netting and looping

Left: 'Barbarossa' 1967 3m × 2m (10′ × 6′9″) Tapestry weaving and pile

Moik Schiele

Moik Schiele is Swiss, was born in Zurich in 1938 and has spent most of her life studying and working there.

In 1957 she became a student in the textile department of the Zurich Kunstgewerbeschule under Elsi Giauque, gaining her diploma in 1961. No doubt she absorbed much of her teacher's concern with the placing of textile and thread constructions in space in a three-dimensional manner.

From 1961 onwards Moik Schiele has mostly worked in her studio in Zurich. She creates large, three-dimensional wovens with clean textures, clear-cut geometric or fluid lines, often of window or ladder-like character. Even when working with an absolutely flat technique her delicate and sensitive feeling for colour helps impart a three-dimensional aspect to the piece. Her technical competence in creating her works is impressive indeed. Smooth tapestry weave broken into a multitude of bars, areas and spaces is often the basic construction.

She has been awarded numerous Swiss major art prizes and her work can be seen in many public buildings, notably in Switzerland but also in the United States. She is featured in the major published works on fibre art and her work has been hung in innumerable international exhibitions, in particular the Lausanne Biennales of 1969,

1971, 1973 and 1975 and major exhibitions in the United States and Britain. Her most recent piece of work, 'Threads in Space', is a new departure for her, both in technique and in its spatial relationships.

'*The aim of my work is to explore as many of the possibilities of weaving as I can, developing, and pursuing them through to their subsequent exhaustion; of new techniques in form, materials—new materials wherever possible—and colour in order to best combine function harmoniously with art (I think of myself primarily as a weaver rather than as an artist) such that—and because a piece is not complete until its hung in that place for which it is designed—the woven elements become integrated maximally in architectural space with the elements of light and air. My work is my life but any particular piece is important to me only so long as it is growing on the loom (I might examine the technical possibility and/or necessities of a work on paper before starting it, but the actual creative process happens on the loom) through to when it is hung. After this it is no longer part of me and I have no further interest in it—my time and interest are focused only on the development of the next piece.*'

Moik Schiele, 1975.

Detailed biography on page 157.

'Copper Wave' 8m × 1.5m (26′3″ × 4′11″) In the Reformiente Kirche, Neu Affoltern
Left: 'Raumelemente' In the Abdankungskapelle, Zurich
Previous page: 'Black Column' 5m × 60cm × 60cm (19′ × 2′ × 2′) (detail) Cotton and chenille
Following page: Piece of work for the Chronischkrankenspiral, Mattenhof, Zurich

Kay Sekimachi

Kay Sekimachi is Japanese-American and was born in San Francisco in 1926, her parents having emigrated to the United States in 1922. She was brought up in the Japanese tradition.

From 1946–1949 she studied at the California College of Arts & Crafts, first painting and design, and then weaving under the tutelage of Trude Guermonprez. In 1950 she began her professional career as a weaver, pursuing her individual development as an artist in fibre and yarn and textile techniques.

In 1956 she returned to the study of weaving, working under Jack Lenor Larsen at Haystack Mountain School in Maine. From 1958 she began to incorporate some teaching into her schedule, mainly in summer-schools. From 1964–1972 she taught at Berkeley Adult School and from 1965 until now at the San Francisco Community College.

Early on in her career she was much moved by the clarity and fluidity of the work of Ruth Asawa. From these seeds she developed an extremely personal weave technique of her own; multi-layered cloth, woven in plain weave and nylon monofilament yarn. The layers interchange and, when removed from the loom, curve and move to create airy, clear, symmetrically organised fluid sculptural shapes. Rather like Peter Collingwood, she pursues her technique and theme again and again, finding ever more variation and meaning.

In a review of her work at an exhibition at the Anneberg Gallery in San Francisco, Barbara Shawcroft wrote, 'Moving around Kay Sekimachi's forms I sense a feeling of quiet flowing delicacy, of infinite beauty in her intertwined, multidimensional layers of black, sometimes white monofilaments, layers that climb in upon each other, forming areas of surprise and wonder.'.

Her fascination with multi-layered weaving (which when removed from the loom can be re-formed) has recently led her to experiment with tubular weaving which resulted in a series of works called 'Marugawas' (round rivers) and most recently to a series of tapestry boxes woven in linen, flat and multi-layered when on the loom but opening out into box-shapes when removed from the loom without further shaping.

Her work is internationally renowned. It is in numerous galleries, private collections and buildings and has been illustrated in many catalogues, publications and books.

In 1974 she was awarded a Craftsman's Fellowship Grant by the National Endowment for the Arts.

Detailed biography on page 158.

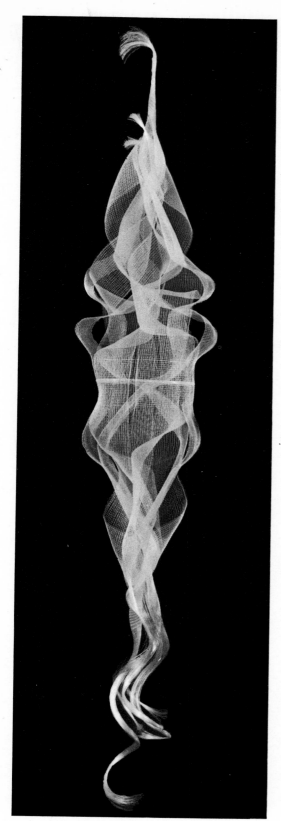

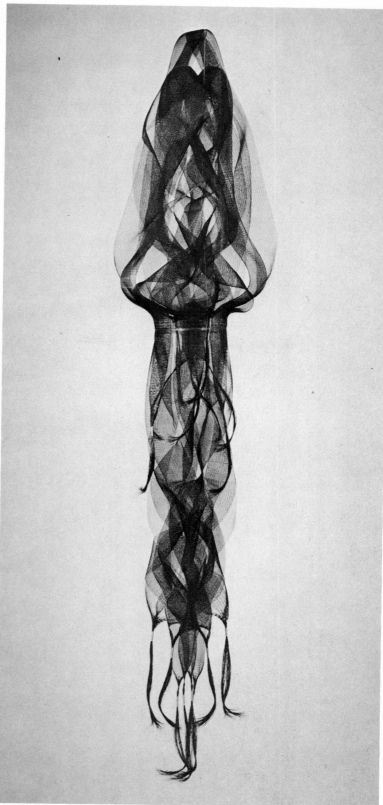

Left: 'Amiyose' 1965 1.5m × 30cm × 30cm (5′ × 1′ × 1′) Quadruple and tubular weave in clear nylon monofilament. Collection Mr and Mrs Kenneth Oberman, Brooklyn, New York

Right: 'Nobori' 1971 2.25m × 46cm (7′6″ × 1′7″) Tubular quadruple weave in black nylon monofilament. Collection Gilbert Baechtold, Lausanne

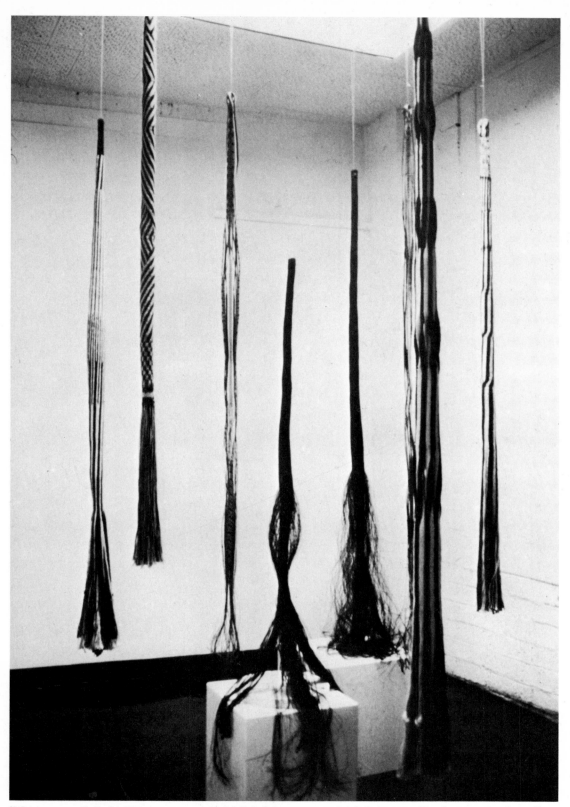

'Marugawa 6' (left) 'Marugawa 7' (middle) 'Marugawa 5' (right) 1972. Card-woven tubes; linen. Collection Royal Scottish Museum, Edinburgh

Far left: 'Amiyose III' 1971 1.7m × 45cm × 42cm (5′5″ × 1′3″ × 1′2″) Quadruple and tubular weave; clear nylon monofilament.

Left: 'Kemuri Katachi' 1970 1.75m × 26cm × 23cm (5′10″ × 10′5″ × 9′5″) Six layered twelve-harness weave; clear nylon monofilament

Sherri Smith

Sherri Smith is American and was born in Chicago in 1943.

She studied at Stanford University, California, obtaining an Honours BA in Art in 1965 and went on to Cranbrook Academy in Michigan where, in 1967, she obtained her Master of Fine Arts degree in Weaving and Textile Design.

There are many facets to the craft of weaving and Sherri Smith is one of those who are eternally intrigued by the complex structures possible with the multi-harness looms. This ability as a pattern weaver made her a 'natural' for her first post, which was designing in the Dorothy Liebes Studio in New York. At this point in her career she was only interested in designing textiles for industry, with no inclination towards anything other than the strictly practical. She then became head of the Woven Design Department at Boris Kroll Fabrics, New York. In 1970 she was awarded a Young Americans Fellowship Grant by the American Crafts Council.

Her work is exhibited copiously in galleries and museums. It consists of complex weave structures, often waffle (or honeycomb) weave, which open out into three-dimensional, space-filling forms of incredible beauty. Their impact has consistently earned them a place at Lausanne, being included in the Biennales of 1971, 1973 and 1975. Her work is illustrated in the major works devoted to the subject of textile fine art. In 1971 she moved to Colorado to teach at Colorado State University. In 1974 she was appointed Assistant Professor of Textiles at the School of Art, University of Michigan in Ann Arbor, where she now lives.

'*I am primarily interested in investigating loom-controlled structures which, while woven flat, expand in some way to fill three-dimensional space. I try to establish big sweeping spaces and movements with both the piece itself and the space it occupies. A piece of my work is typically composed of many loom-woven modular pieces, either sandwiched together or assembled in some other way. I find the organic forms which result from the use of these highly ordered and ridgedly geometric modules to be very exciting. I also react strongly to the heavy, rather opulent massing of yarn which is often used in contrast to very lacy open places in the same work.*

I work on multi-harness looms, a twenty-five shaft dobby and a twenty shaft treadle loom. I weave with mohair, wool, metallic guimpe, rayon and occasionally jute and find that yarns with a somewhat luxurious handle most effective. I dye all the coloured yarns I use myself.'
Sherri Smith, 1975.

Detailed biography on page 158.

'Mushroom' 1972 1.8m × 1.8m × 90cm (6′ × 6′ × 3′) Waffle (honeycomb) weave; mohair

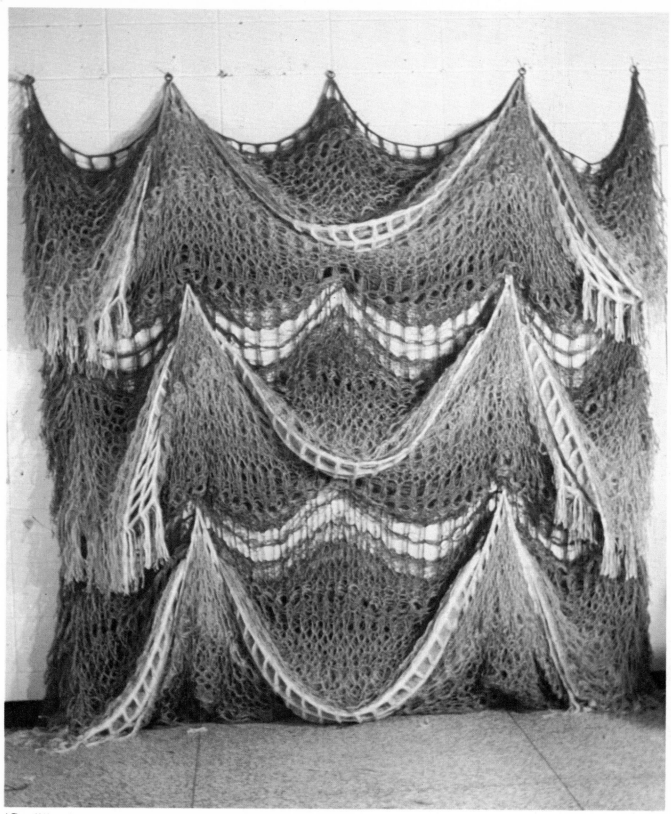

'Cordillera' 1974 2.4m × 2.4m (8′ × 8′) Waffle weave; mohair

Left: 'Thorne' 2.25m × 2.25m × 1.6m (7′6″ × 7′6″ × 4′) Waffle weave; mohair

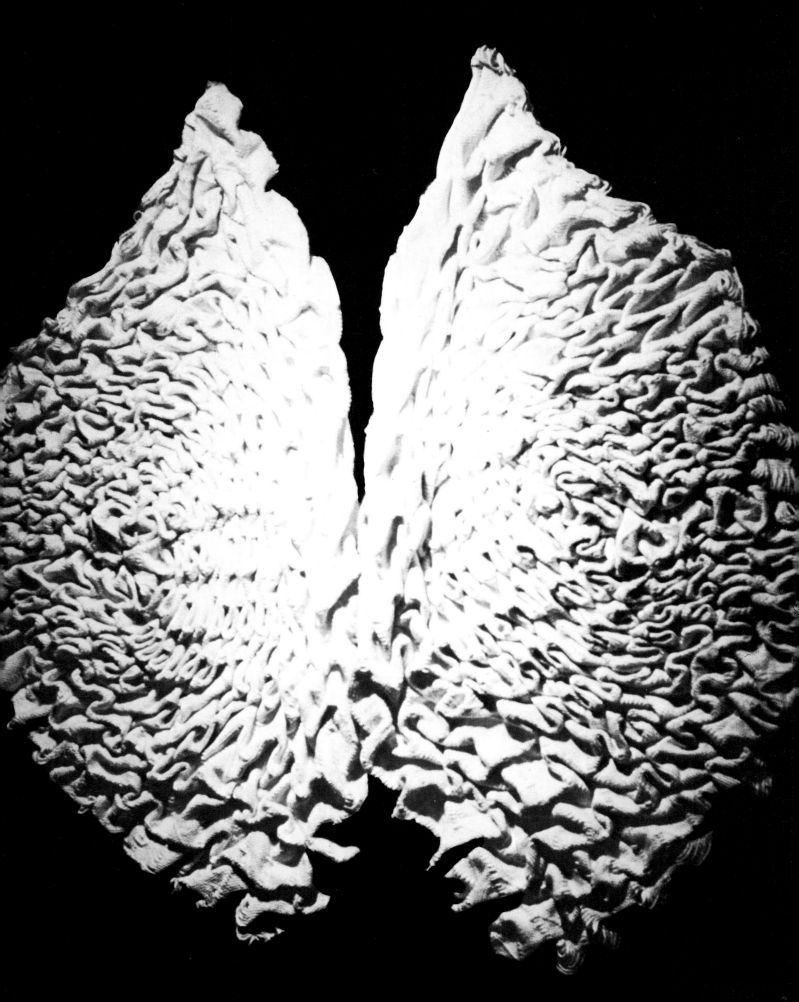

'Silver Lining' 2.25m × 1.8m × 45cm (7′6″ × 6′ × 1′6″)

Left : 'New Moon, Old Moon' 1973 2.4m × 2.4m (8′ × 8′) Waffle (honeycomb) weave; rayon

Inge Vahle

Inge Vahle is German and was born in the small village of Krevese, Altmark in 1915. The vast open landscape of this area, with its farms, windmills, castles and rivers has influenced her always.

Between 1934 and 1938 she studied painting at the Academies of Berlin and Dusseldorf and at this time she met her husband, Fritz, also a painter. The two of them worked together, painting, drawing, writing and travelling.

They live in Darmstadt and for periods of concentrated work and solitude retreat to an island where the ships, rocks, nets and all the atmosphere that the sea projects help them to work. Many of Inge Vahle's textile objects are conceived here. She enjoys natural history and visits archaeological museums to study natural form and the process of growth which she finds constantly surprising and energising.

In her works she is concerned with 'the problem of technical evolution, the progress of intellectual order and the danger of explosion'. Her main material is sisal, often in blacks or sombre browns. She uses, among other elements, wrapped and wound spools embedded in and contrasting with violent outgrowths and cascades of yarn. She incorporates also 'found objects', wood, tubing and metal. The works are huge, towering and have incredible impact. They impart a sense of terrible menace but are subtly softened by references to the content and structure of natural form.

They are totally related to the architectural spaces in which they are set, churches, theatres, museums and other public buildings. They have been widely illustrated in books on art but probably because her work is mainly firmly set in European buildings, Inge Vahle is much better known in her native Europe than in Britain and America.

'One asks the question, "Why does one work, why does one work so hard, why does one exhibit one's work, and why does one work with textile means?". The answer is this—everyone is an individual and has different matters, on which he feels compelled to comment. But the media in which he will best comment, each person must decide for himself, according to his requirements and his abilities.

I began as a painter but soon found that the media which best expressed my will was brittle hemp and sisal. Black is the colour which best welds the material into an homogeneous whole of plastic and graphic reliefs. I prepare all my material in its various forms right at the beginning of any piece of work so that all is ready to be used spontaneously and without hindrance, to give substance to ideas which may be held in my mind or I may have noted down in a verbal sketch.

My textile objects depict movement, change and unrest. I am

fascinated by one's day to day experience of the menace lurking in human events and in technological progress. I use a set of formulas, repeats of knotted surfaces and wound spools which dissolve and fall out of order because of unexpected developments.'
Inge Vahle, Darmstadt, 1975

Detailed biography on page 158.

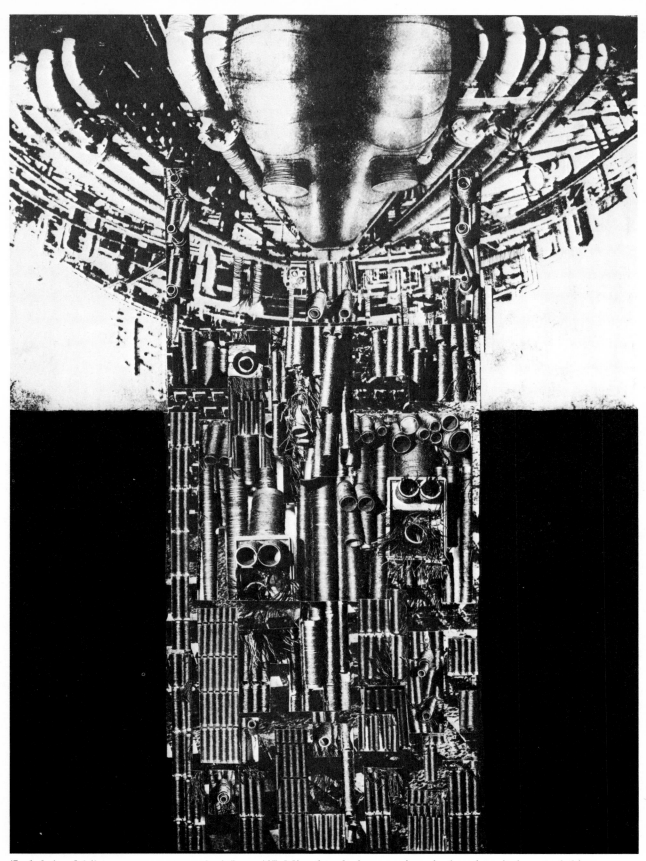

'Induktionfeld' 1973 5.4m × 3.5m (17′9″ × 11′6″) Mixed techniques using sisal and varied materials

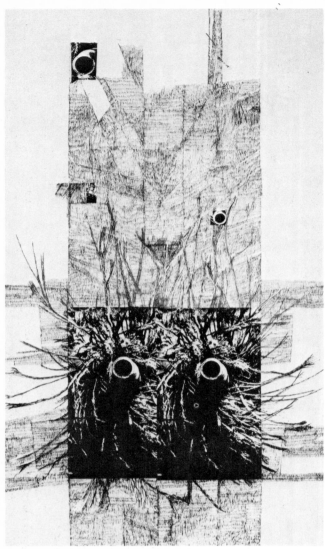

'Unexpected Evolution' 1m × 65cm (3'4″ × 2'2″) Collage
Right : 'Unexpected Evolution' 1m × 65cm (3'4″ × 2'2″)
Collage

'Energieschema' 2.7m × 3m × 60cm (9′ × 10′ × 2′)

Left: 'Stabehuk' (detail)
Details of works in black sisal using found objects, cylinders and wood

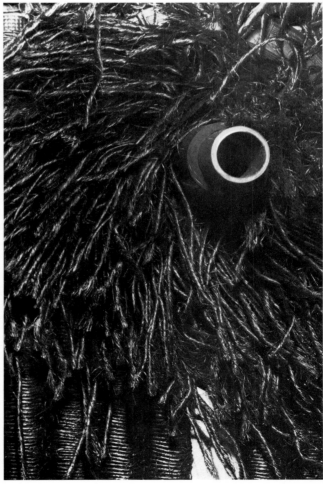

Jindřich Vohánka

Jindřich Vohánka is Czechoslovakian and was born in Picin in 1922.

He, like the other two great Czech weavers, Mzarek and Tichy, produces shaped weavings, with little three-dimensionality, all the impact being in the flat shape alone, together with the movement of the threads within it. He studied at the School of Textiles in Brno between 1938 and 1941. Then the war intervened. In 1949 he returned to his studies, this time at the School of Decorative Arts in Prague under Professor Kybal, obtaining his Masters Degree in 1954.

From 1955 to 1962 he was artistic director of the Umelecká Remesla tapestry studios at Valašské Meziřiči and in 1962 became Professor of Textiles at his original School in Brno where he is still.

He says 'only the spiritual matters, the material is unimportant' and his philosophy is clear from the depth of meaning which emanates from his works, all of which are produced by the artist himself with no helpers. All the work is about man's relationship to his god and to the universe and Vohánka endeavours to speak to us through the medium of tapestry as the medieval tapestry weavers did to their contemporaries. Thoughts spring from the Old and New Testaments and writings such as the Revelation of St John as depicted in the 'Apocalypse d'Angers'. Vohánka fixes spiritual man firmly in his contemporary situation with oblique reference to space, flight and science fiction. The means by which Vohánka attains his artistic, philosophical and spiritual messages are masterly. The shaped weaving is produced by the most careful, intricate and concentrated manipulation and moving around of the warp-ends and the weft. They converge, spread out, move elsewhere and converge again. The edges follow the flow and are an all-important element.

He has participated in numerous exhibitions in his own country and his work has reached a wider public at important international exhibitions like Expo '58 in Brussels, Lausanne Biennale of 1967, Perspektif in Textiel in Amsterdam 1969, and the Biennal of São Paulo in 1973.

His work is not as widely illustrated and publicised as it deserves as Vohánka is totally uninterested in exposure and such is the subtlety and importance of his message that he is wary of being misinterpreted.

The following are extracts from a long statement by Vohánka.

About natural and found materials:
'. . . a bit of charred rag which bears the trace of its own tragic history can recall the atomic horrors of Hiroshima more effectively than the most expertly machine woven wool . . .

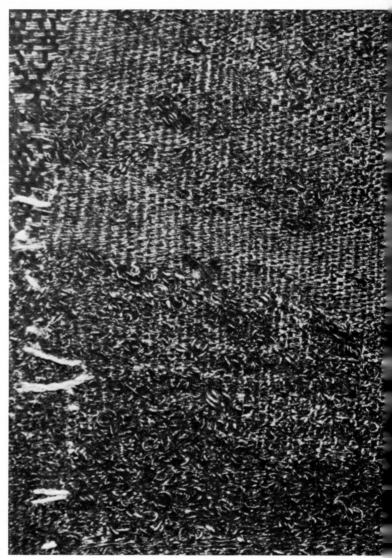

Buffalo skins with paintings organically incorporated by North American Indians, tufts of human hair and parrot feathers inserted into religious objects—what overwhelming statements by materials! Where is man as an author in all this? Is he simply the will and vital force of these organisms, or are these often valueless materials only a pile of refuse? Numerous objects seen at the Lausanne Biennales have taught us to understand that raw fleece, rope bleached by sun and unravelled by wind and water, wire and metal, all have much to tell us.'

About new techniques:
'We are beginning to discover that a large number of techniques for improving things sometimes forcibly imposed on materials and equipment often deprive them of beauty instead of conferring it.'

About the new 'Fibre Art' works:
'in the process of their construction the creators often appear to be no more than the vital force and the unifying will necessary to the organisation of the 'biological' structure of the work,

which is based on new feelings and on aesthetic principles which differ fundamentally not only from the aesthetics of say painting but also from all former concepts of tapestry.'

About the new materials:

'It is true that the mere discovery of new materials is not sufficient to create a work of art, but the use of them marks the sincerity and validity of contemporary thought, even though our progress is uncertain and stumbling.'

About traditional techniques:

'Once freedom is obtained from ideological slavery to the many technical processes which exist anonymously in a work of art, at the most as hidden tectonic components, then the image of our world will widen out and man's feelings will be greatly enriched. Though we must remember that often our use of our technical skills and our respective handling of materials has in its very essence the seeds of the aesthetic already, or why in a highly technical and specialised journal do we come across phrases like 'twisting should preserve the maximum of softness in the thread'? It would also seem that very basic chores of

textile production, the warping, winding and so on, all have a functional role in the artist's progress towards a total art-work. The link between the technical construction of a piece of work and its aesthetic message and context are of seminal importance and indissoluble.

A summing up of his reflections on contemporary tapestry:

1. There is total rejection of the 'narrative picture' tapestry.
2. All the components in the creation of a work are indissolubly bound together, the technical with the aesthetic.
3. These components have been emancipated from all traditional concepts.
4. The whole art form is autonomous, owing nothing to other fine art media.
5. The artists are an anonymous vital force and the work's growth and birth are governed by its own "natural" laws.'

Jindřich Vohánka

Detailed biography on page 159.

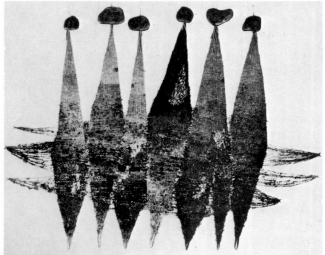

'La Rêve de Monsieur Blériot' 1965 2.4m × 4.6m
(7′10″ × 15′1″) High warp tapestry; sisal, wool, padding.
Collection National Gallery of Prague

Left: 'L'An 1922' 1967 3m × 4m (10′ × 13′1″) High warp
tapestry; sisal, wool, metal, wood. Collection National
Gallery of Prague

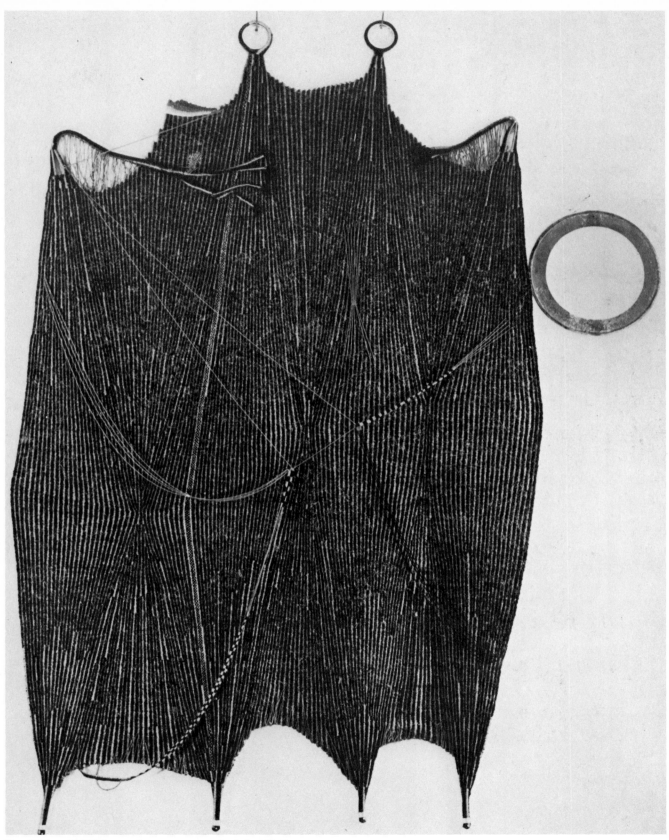

'La Visite d'Aldebaran' 3.1m × 1.9m (10′2″ × 6′4″)

Susan Weitzman

Susan Weitzman was born in Pennsylvania in 1931 and lives in New York with her husband, daughter and son. She received her BA in Painting at Smith College in Massachussetts in 1953 and her MA in Art Education at New York University in 1958.

Lenore Tawney was an early and sustaining influence on her and the two have in common an absolute purity of artistic and intellectual intent.

Susan Weitzman's first works were executed in tapestry techniques. The work became smaller with each successive piece, finally ending in the miniature. Then there came a moment when she discovered that the quality of a particular hand-spun warp with which she was working showed no need of a weft at all—so weft was abandoned and from then on ideas were given substance solely through the use of the limitless subtleties of yarn thickness, twist and variations, the spinning being produced with the drop-spindle.

She works very slowly and with extreme deliberation, sometimes output flows, sometimes it moves slowly or stops completely. She is obviously fascinated by the simple perfection of the circle, which is the main and often the only image in most of her work, occasionally juxtaposed with the square. Thus, she produces her gentle variations on the circle theme by means of the hand-spun thread only, with the subtlest of twist-changes. The resulting works are delicate, compelling compositions of simplicity and enormous subtlety. Her work has been illustrated in most of the publications on fibre art and is in museums and private collections.

She feels little need at the moment to express herself in visual terms as she is deeply involved with the organisation and running of a centre for meditation in New York but one must hope that an artist of such rare skill and eloquence will return to the use of fibre and yarn as a means of communication soon.

Detailed biography on page 159.

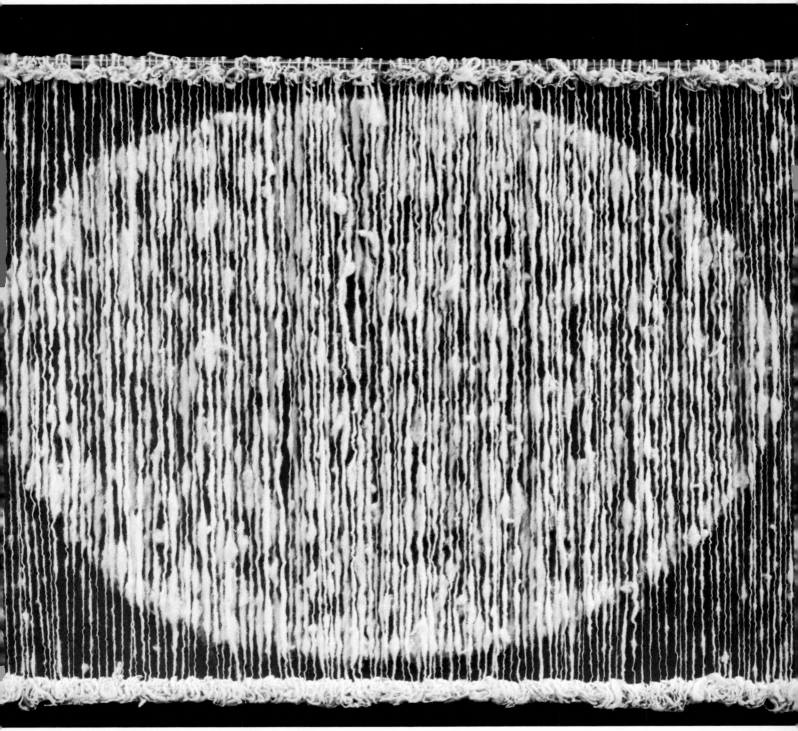

'Ancient Traditional Form' 1970 85cm × 45cm (2′10″ × 1′6″) Handspun wool; exposed warp with differential of twist. Collection Mr and Mrs Joel Berson

'Homage to Lenore Tawney' 1968 2.1m × 2.1m (7′ × 7′) Two layers of exposed warp; handspun natural wool
Left: 'Homage to Lenore Tawney' Photographed in a different light

'To Shyam' 1970 3m × 1.2m (10′ × 4′) Two layers of exposed warp; natural brown and white wool with some dyed ink areas

Right : 'Tapestry for Frances Lynn' 1967 73cm × 53cm (2′5″ × 1′9″) Handspun natural wool; exposed warp with differential of twist. Collection Museum of Modern Art, New York

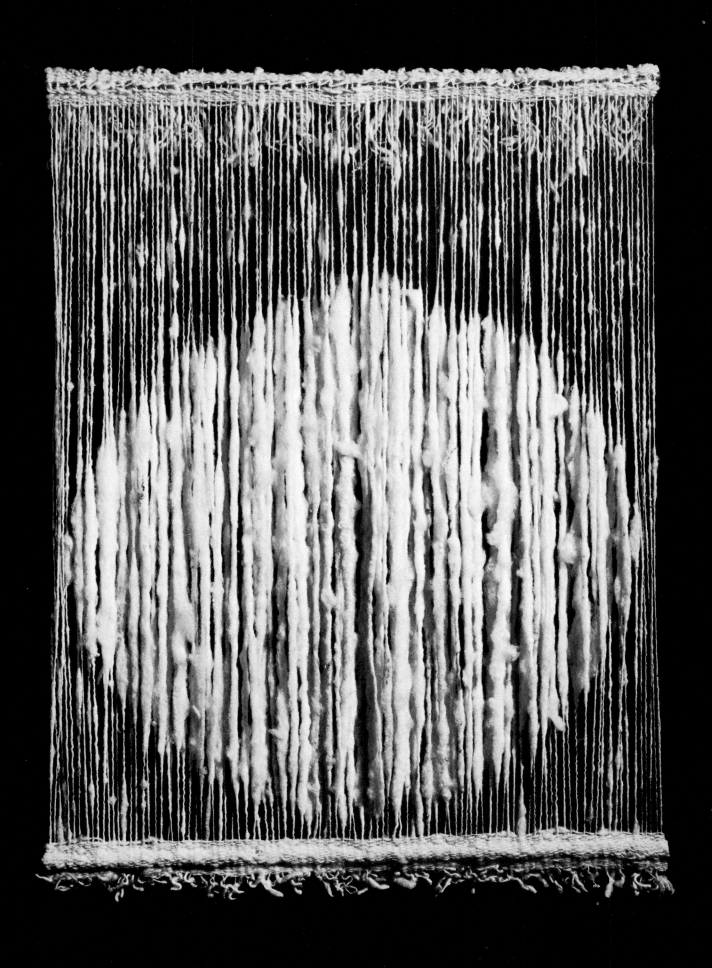

Claire Zeisler

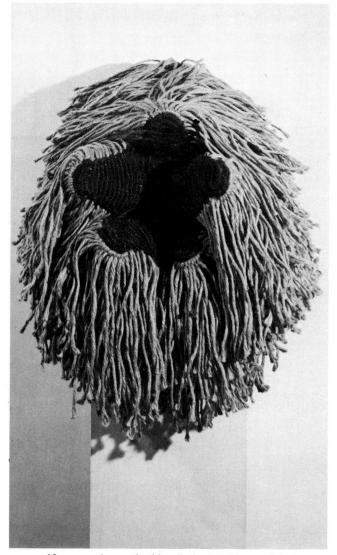

Claire Zeisler is American and was born in Cincinatti, Ohio, in 1903. She studied drawing and painting in Cincinatti then went to Columbia University, New York, to study design and finally for a further two years at the Bauhaus-based Chicago School of Design.

She did not take up weaving until later and is self-taught in this field and also in the field of off-loom techniques to which she gradually turned. Research is of the utmost importance to her and in Claire Zeisler's scheme of things 'self-taught' means that she followed her own dictum which is, 'one must know the technique or techniques from every point in order to become master of it, which means making it your own and which is the key to interesting work'.

She started exhibiting in 1960 and her work was part of the very important 'Woven Forms' Exhibition in 1962 at the Museum of Contemporary Crafts, which was the first of its kind. This was followed by another innovative participatory exhibition in 1963 at the Kunstgewerbe-museum, Zurich, which was one of the first times modern 'tapestries' from the States were shown in Europe. It was at this time that she moved into experiments with off-loom techniques—many of them. She opened a workshop in Chicago in 1967 which she kept until 1973 and during that time she taught at the Art Institute of Chicago. Since 1973 she prefers to work in the studio attached to her apartment,

a magnificent eyrie overlooking Lake Michigan with the sky, the lake and the immense sweep of Lakeshore Drive and its beautiful high-rise architecture. At night it is a world of darkness, lights and water. Her works are dense, impressive, self-contained presences. She was one of the first artists to work in a sculptural fashion in that many of her works are free-standing forms. They are not supported by armatures. The techniques she uses in each piece of work are indissolubly part of but then totally subservient to the overriding form. In the last few years, she has turned her attention from the large to the smaller and from techniques to ideas, the symbolism of cloaks, coats and body-wrappings for instance and is using very natural, basic, untreated materials.

She is internationally known, is featured in all great works on the fibre-art movement and her work is in public buildings, museums and collections world-wide.

Detailed biography on page 159.

'Sunday Presence' 1968 1.8m high × 2.1m wide (6′ × 7′) Red and white jute and wool

Right: 'Cascade' 1969 75cm (30″) high. Natural jute; a free-standing macramé knotted and bound shape with no structural support. Collection Dr Robert Sager, Peoria, Illinois.

Left: 'Untitled' 76 cm (30″) Natural jute and black jute

'Slinky' 2.7m (9′) high. Three shades of red cotton; 24 wrapped coils *Left*: detail

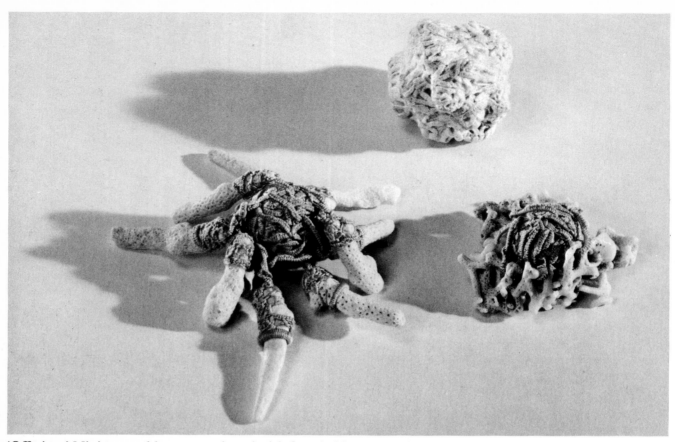

'Offerings' Miniatures: blue cotton thread with found objects; looped stitch

'Family of Balls', Miniature 1973 Red cottons

'Black Madagascar' 1972 2.4m × 65cm × 30cm
(8′ × 2′2″ × 1′) Wall hanging in black jute and natural
raffia

'Red Madagascar' 1972 2.3m × 65cm × 30cm
(7′8″ × 2′2″ × 1′) Wall hanging in red jute and natural
raffia

Detailed Biographies

* indicates an individual or one-man exhibition

Magdalena Abakanowicz

Biographical details

1930	Born in Falenty, Poland
1950–55	Studies Painting and Sculpture at the Fine Art Academy, Warsaw
1965	Award of the Biennale, São Paulo The Great Award of the Minister of Culture, Poland
1965	Teaches at the Academy of Fine Arts, Posnan, where she is now Professor
1967	The Award of the Polish Artists' Union
1972	The Great Award of the Folk Republic, Poland
1974	Receives the degree of Doctor *honoris causa*, Royal College of Art, London

Some important exhibitions

1960	Exhibition, Gallery Kordegarda, Warsaw*
1962	Galerie Dautzenberg, Paris*; Biennale International de la Tapisserie Contemporaine, Lausanne (and all subsequent Biennales)
1965	Galeria Zachenta, Warsaw,* 2 Biennale, São Paulo, Brazil
1967	Galerie Pauli, Lausanne*
1969	'Perspectief in Textiel', Stedelijk Museum, Amsterdam
1968	Biennale, Venice; Kunstmuseum 'Helmhaus', Zurich*
1970	Nationalmuseum, Stockholm*; Södertalje Kunsthall, Södertalje
1969	'Wall Hanging Exhibition', Museum of Modern Art, New York
1971	Pasdena Art Museum, USA*
1972	Kunsthalle, Düsseldorf* Edinburgh Festival of Arts, Edinburgh
1973	Arnolfini Gallery, Bristol*; Galerie d'Art Moderne, Bordeaux*
1974	'Poland Today', Museums of Science and Technology, Detroit and San Francisco
1975	Whitechapel Gallery, London

Work included in following collections

Nationalmuseum, Warsaw
Stedelijk Museum, Amsterdam
The Museum of Modern Art, New York
Museo de Arte Moderna, São Paulo
Nationalmuseum, Stockholm
Kunstindustrimuseet, Oslo
Museum Bellerive, Zurich
Naredni Museum, Prague
Frans Halsmuseum, Haarlem
Kunsthalle, Mannheim
Museo Español de Arte Contemporáneo, Madrid

Olga de Amaral

Biographical details

1932	Born in Bogotá, Colombia
1951–52	Studies Architecture at the Colegio Mayor de Cundinamarca
1954–55	Studies Textiles at Cranbrook Academy of Arts, Michigan
1963	Is appointed Director of Architectural Design, Universidad de Los Andes, Bogotá
1966–72	Director of Textiles, Universidad de Los Andes
1968–72	Colombian representative at the 'World Crafts Council'
1970	Established her own studio workshop in Bogotá
1970–74	Director for Latin America of the 'World Crafts Council'
1974–	Awarded Guggenheim Fellowship. Lives in Paris with regular working spells in Bogotá

Some important exhibitions

1959	Exhibition, Sociedad Colombiana de Arquitectos, Bogotá*
1966	Museo de Bellas Artes, Caracas*
1967, 71	Three individual exhibitions in the USA
1969	'Wall hangings', Museum of Modern Art, New York
1970	Museum of Contemporary Crafts, New York City*
1971	Zacheta Gallery, Warsaw
1970, 71	'Textile Constructions' Gallery Ruth Kaufmann, New York City 'Deliberate Entanglements' travelling exhibition to Los Angeles, Vancouver, Utah, Chicago
73, 75	'Biennale Internationale de la Tapisserie Contemporaine', Lausanne
1973	'Woven Walls' Gallery La Demeure, Paris '32 Artistas Colombianos', Museo de Arte Moderno, Bogotá Exhibition, La Banque Nationale de Paris, Paris*
1974, 75	Galerie Rivolta, Lausanne*
1975	'History of Colombian Art' Petit Palais, Paris Bonython Gallery, Sydney* South Yarra Gallery, Melbourne* Artweave Textile Gallery, New York
1976	'2nd International Exhibition of Miniature Textiles', British Crafts Centre, London

Work included in the following collections

Dreyfus Corporation, New York City
Regency Hyatt House, Chicago
Braniff, Kansas
First National City Bank, Chicago
Embarcadero Center, San Francisco
Fort Worth National Bank, Fort Worth, Texas
Museo de Arte Moderno, Bogotá
Colección 'Colcultura', Bogotá
Colección 'Coltejer', Medellín, Colombia
The Chicago Art Institute, Chicago
Peachtree Centre, Atlanta, Georgia

Tadek Beutlich

Biographical information

Born in Lwowek, Poland

1922	Studies Drawing and Painting in Poland, Germany and Italy

1922 Studies Drawing and Painting in Poland, Germany and Italy

1947 Comes to England and attends the Sir John Cass School of Art

1948 Begins weaving and attends Camberwell School of Art

1951–74 Teaches and gives lectures at Camberwell School of Art

1967 Moves to 'Gospels', Sussex, once the studio of Ethel Mairet

1967 Publishes 'Technique of Woven Tapestry'

1973 Moves to Spain where he now lives and works

Some important exhibitions

1963, 67, 69, 72 Exhibitions, Grabowski Gallery, London*

1971, 73 Croneen Gallery, Sydney and Melbourne

1967, 69 Biennale Internationale de la Tapisserie Contemporaine, Lausanne

1970 'British Designer Craftsmen', Smithsonian Institution, Washington DC

1971 'Deliberate Entanglements' travelling exhibition, Los Angeles
Modern British Hangings, Scottish Arts Council Gallery, Edinburgh

1972 'Fibre Structures', Denver Art Museum

1973 'The Craftsman's Art' Victoria and Albert Museum, London

1974, 76 'International Exhibition of Miniature Textiles', British Crafts Centre, London

Jagoda Buić

Biographical details

1930 Born in Split, Dalmatia

1949 Studies History of Art, University of Zagreb
Travels and studies in Italy
Works with costume and decor at Cinecittà, Rome

1953–54 Studies tapestry and theatre decor at the Academy of Applied Arts, Vienna

1955 Silver Medal, Triennale, Milan

1961 First Prize for textile Design, International Exhibition for Design, Belgrade

1965– First Prize for Yugoslavian wall hangings, Sombor
Travels in Europe, Canada, the United States, South America
Participates in major textile exhibitions and projects

1975 Art Prize, São Paulo Biennale, Brazil

Some important exhibitions

1954 Triennale, Milan

1965, 67, 69, 71, 73, 75 'Biennale Internationale de la Tapisserie Contemporaine', Lausanne

1966 Museum of Applied Arts, Zagreb

1967 Expo 67, Montreal
Biennale, São Paulo

1968, 70 Biennale, Venice

1969 'Perspectief in Textiel', Stedelijk Museum, Amsterdam
'Wall Hangings', Museum of Modern Art, New York
Galleria Pauli, Lausanne*

1971 'Rosc' (Poetry of Vision), Dublin

1972 One-woman exhibitions in the museums of Split, Dubrovnik and Ljubliana*

1974 Museé d'Art Moderne, Belgrade (also Paris)

1975 Formes Tissées, Musée d'Art Moderne, Paris

1976 'Jagoda Buic', Musée de Nantes*

Work included in the following collections

Kennedy Center for the Performing Arts, Washington DC
Dreyfus Fund Collection, New York City
Continental Bank Inc., New York City
Stedelijk Museum, Amsterdam
In museums and art galleries in Bordeaux, Paris, Nuremburg, Lausanne, Sarajevo, Split and Zagreb.

Barbara Chase-Riboud

Biographical details

1939 Born in Philadelphia, Pennsylvania
Studies at the Tyler School of Fine Arts, Temple University

1958 John Hay Whitney Fellowships (Sculpture) Studies in Rome

1960 Studies at Yale University School of Art and Architecture under Rico Lebrun and Josef Albers M.F.A. Degrees Meets Sheila Hicks
Is influenced by Eastern and African cultures
Travels to North Africa, China and India, Egypt and Turkey

1961 Moves to Paris

1973 National Endowment for the Arts Individual Grant

Some important exhibitions

1966 Exhibition of drawings, Cadran Solaire, Paris*

1970 The Massachusetts Institute of Technology, Boston*
Bertha Schaefer Gallery, New York*

1972 Betty Parsons Gallery, New York City*

1973 Institute of Contemporary Arts, Philadelphia*
University Museum, Berkeley

1973 The Merian Gallery, Krefeld, West Germany*

1973 The Kunstmuseum, Düsseldorf, West Germany*
Recurring exhibitions at the Whitney Museum, New York

Work included in the following collections

The Museum of Modern Art, New York City
The University Museum, Berkeley, California
The Metropolitan Museum of Art, New York City
The Newark Museum, Newark, USA
Centre National des Arts Contemporains, Paris
The Geigy Foundation, New York
The Kenton Corporation, New York
The Philadelphia Art Alliance, Philadelphia
The Wheaton Plaza Fountain, Washington, USA

Peter Collingwood

Biographical details

1922 Born in London

1946 Qualified in Medicine at St Mary's Hospital Medical School, London

1946–48 Serves in the Army

1949 Works as a Doctor for the Red Cross

1950 Begins training in the weaving studios of Ethel Mairet and Barbara Sawyer, Sussex
Moves to Carlisle, works with Alastair Morton
1052 Establishes own workshop in Highgate, London
First one-man exhibition at Heal's, London
1958 Moves to Digswell House Arts Centre, Welwyn Garden City
1963 Gold Medal, International Handicrafts Exhibition, Munich
1964– Moves to Nayland, Essex, where he lives and works. Teaches in the United States and at Farnham School of Art, England
1968 Publishes 'The Techniques of Rug Weaving' (Faber & Faber)
1974 Published 'The Techniques of Sprang' (Faber & Faber)
Awarded C.A.C. grant for research on tablet weaving
Awarded OBE for his work as a weaver

Some important exhibitions

1954 Group exhibition, Heal's, London
1964, 73 British Crafts Centre, London*
1966 Building Centre, London*
1969 Victoria and Albert Museum, London (with Hans Coper)
1971 'Three British Weavers', travelling exhibition, USA
1971, 73 Denis Croneen Gallery, Sydney*
1972 'Fabrications', Detroit
1973 'The Craftsman's Art', Victoria and Albert Museum, London
1974 'In Praise of Hands', Ontario Science Centre, Toronto
1975 Kunstindustrimuseum, Copenhagen
Kunstindustrimuseum, Oslo
British Crafts Centre, London

Work included in the following collections
Victoria and Albert Museum, London
Shell Centre, London
New Zealand House, London
Selwyn College, Cambridge
University of York
Metropolitan Cathedral, Liverpool
National and Grindlays, London
National Gallery of Melbourne
National Westminster Bank, Manchester
University of Liverpool
National Museum of Wales, Cardiff
Crafts Study Centre, Bath
Public Library, Welwyn Garden City
Froebel Institute, London
City Art Gallery, Bristol

Daniel Graffin

Biographical details

1938 Born in Paris
1955 Studies at the School of Art, London Polytechnic
1957–58 Studies painting with Aujame and L'hote
1960 Diplôme des Métiers d'Art
1963 Travels to Egypt. Begins to weave and studies

natural dyeing in the workshop of the architect Wissa Wassef
1964 Returns to France to work in tapestry
1973 Establishes his own studio in Paris

Some important exhibitions

1973, 75 Biennale Internationale de la Tapisserie Contemporaine, Lausanne
1974 Suzy Langlois Gallery, Paris
Museum of Contemporary Crafts, New York
1974, 76 International Exhibition of Miniature Textiles, British Crafts Centre, London
Govett-Brewster Gallery, New Plymouth, New Zealand
1975 Tapisseries Nouvelles, Musée des Arts Decoratifs, Paris
1976 Musée de Nantes

Work included in the following collections
American Telephone and Telegraph Company

Josep Grau-Garriga

Biographical details

1929 Born in Sant Cugat del Vallés, Barcelona, Spain
1943-47 Studies graphics and interior design at L'Escola d'Arts i Oficis in Barcelona
1947-51 Studies painting and engraving at the School of Fine Arts in Barcelona Travels throughout Spain
1953-54 Works and exhibits as a painter and engraver
1957 Begins working with tapestries
1958-59 Travels extensively in Europe Lives in Paris where he works with Jean Lurçat Serves as Artistic Director at the Escola Catalana de Tapis at Sant Cugat del Vallés First tapestries using various materials and textures
1959-76 Travels and exhibits in Europe and in the United States
1969 Receives a grant from the International Institute of Education in New York to visit centres of art education in the United States, Canada and Mexico

Some important exhibitions

1962 European Contemporary Tapestries, Chicago
1965, 67, 69 Biennale Internationale de la Tapisserie, Lausanne
1964, 66 Biennale d'Art Sacré, Salzburg
1967 Il Bienal Internacional de Arte Applicado, Uruguay
'Contemporary European Tapestries', travelling exhibition, USA
IX Biennale d'Arte, São Paulo
1968, 70, 72, 74 Galerie La Demeure, Paris*
1968 Arte Espanol Actuel, Brazil
'Contemporary Tapestries', IBM, New York
1969 19th Salon de l'Art Sacré, Musée de l'Art Moderne, Paris
1971, 73 Arras Gallery, New York*
1972 'Fibre Structures', Denver Art Museum
1973 State University, New York*
International Institute of Education, New York*
1973 'Hard & Soft', Arras Gallery, New York

1974 Chapitre de la Tapisserie, Clos-Vougeot
His work has been, and is being, constantly
exhibited in galleries all over Spain

Work included in the following collections
Monastery of Sant Cugat del Valles
La Selva del Camp, Tarragona
Church of the Virgin del Pilar, Barcelona
Church of Santa Maria, Cornella
Church of Sant Antoni Ma Claret, Sallent
Church of Santa Maria de Salon, Tarragona
Church of Santa Julia d'Argentona, Barcelona

Françoise Grossen

Biographical details

1943 Born in Neuchatel, Switzerland
1962–63 Bacclaureat Scientifique, School of Architecture of
the Polytechnical University in Lausanne Travels
to Africa and is strongly influenced by African
culture In 1964 participates in the exhibition
'Gewebte Formen' at the Kunstgewerbemuseum
in Zurich, together with Sheila Hicks, Claire
Zeisler, Lenore Tawney
1967 Graduates in Textile Design from the School of
Arts and Crafts, Basle
1968 Moves to California to study Textile Design with
Professor Bernard Kester
1969 Obtains her Master of Arts degree from the
University of California, Los Angeles
1969–70 Works as textile designer at the Larsen Design
Studio
1971–73 Appointed instructor of Weaving and Macramé at
the New School, New York City, and at the Art
School of the Brooklyn Museum, Brooklyn, NY
1973–76 Begins to concentrate on her own work, with brief
teaching spells at summer schools and workshops
in the United States Receives commissions from
architects

Some important exhibitions

1968 First group show, 'Objects Are?', Museum of
Contemporary Crafts, New York City
1969 'Wall Hangings', Museum of Modern Art, New
York
1971 Deliberate Entanglements, Los Angeles
1969, 71, 73, 'Biennale Internationale de la Tapisserie
75 Contemporaine', Lausanne
1974 '1st International Exhibition of Miniature Textiles'
London, Zurich, Lausanne
'In Praise of Hands', Ontario Science Centre,
Toronto
1972 Sculpture in Fibre, Museum of Contemporary
Crafts, New York

Work included in the following collections
Mrs A Feinberg, New York
Mrs J Kaplan, New York
Jack Larsen, New York
Dreyfus Fund, GM Building, New York
O'Hare Regency Hyatt House, Chicago
One Embarcadero Center, San Francisco
Embarcadero Regency Hyatt, San Francisco

Bank of Texas, San Antonio
Bellerive Museum, Zurich

Ted Hallman

Biographical details

1933 Born in Bucks County, Pennsylvania
1956 Graduates as Bachelor of Fine Arts and Bachelor
Sc. Education at Tyler School of Fine Arts,
Temple University, Philadelphia
1958 M.F.A. in Painting and M.F.A. in Textile Design
at Cranbrook Academy of Art, Michigan
1958–62 Works as a designer for the textile industry and for
interior designers and architects and teaches
1962 Awarded the L.C. Tiffany Grant for study in Austria
1963–68 Head of Textile Department at Moore College of
Art, Philadelphia Textile consultant to Jamaica for
the United Nations
1970–74 Full-time study for a Ph.D. in Education at
Berkeley University of California
1975 Professor of Textiles at San José State College,
California

Some important exhibitions

1958 First exhibition in 'Young Americans', Museum
of Contemporary Crafts New York
1960 Internationales Kunsthandwerk, Stuttgart
1962 'Modern American Wallhangings', Victoria and
Albert Museum, London
1964 Milan Triennale
1972 'Objects USA' international travelling exhibition
1974 '1st International Exhibition of Miniature Textiles',
British Crafts Centre, London

Work included in the following collections
Victoria and Albert Museum, London
Brooklyn Museum of Art, New York
Cooper Hewitt Museum, New York
Smithsonian Institution, Washington D.C.
Philadelphia Museum of Art, California
Museum of Contemporary Crafts, New York
Addison Gallery of American Art, Andover, Massachussets

Sheila Hicks

Biographical details

1934 Born in Hastings, Nebraska
1945–52 Studies in Detroit, Michigan, and Winnetka,
Illinois Begins to paint
1952–54 Syracuse University. Studies printmaking, Greek
mythology Visits Mexico Begins photographing
1954–57 Yale University Studies with Josef Albers, George
Kubler Meets Anni Albers, Louis Kahn, Junius
Bird Weaves miniatures Writes B.F.A. thesis in
pre-Columbian textiles
1957–59 Fulbright scholarship to Chile Travels through
Colombia, Ecuador, Peru, Bolivia, Brazil Returns
to Yale University where she studies painting and
drawing with Rico Lebrun
1959 M.F.A. First marriage First visit to Europe with
Fribourg Grant Experiments with three-
dimensional thread structures

1960–63 Lives in Mexico Meets architect Luis Barragan and sculptor Matias Goeritz Weaves monochrome panels. Teaches design at Universidad de Mexioo

1964–65 Lives in Europe and conducts seminars on thread exploration in Germany and England

1965 Marries the Chilean painter Zañartu and moves to Paris Establishes her studio 'Atelier des Grands Augustins'

1966–70 Collaborates with architect Warren Platner, executes important commissions, establishes workshops in India and Taller Huaquen studio in Chile. Works in Morocco

1971–75 Experiments with thread wrapped around neon light Founds 'Taller Los Bravos' in Mexico, with Legorreta and Barragan Works in India with Daniel Graffin In 1974 receives the AIA gold medal for craftsmanship

Some important exhibitions

1958 Museum of Fine Arts, Santiago, Chile

1964 'Gewebte Formen', Kunstgewerbemuseum, Zurich

1967, 69, 71, 'Biennale Internationale de la Tapisserie Moderne', 73, 75 Lausanne

1969 'Perspectief in Textiel', Stedelijk Museum, Amsterdam 'Wall Hangings', Museum of Modern Art, New York

1970 Exhibition, Bab Rouah National Museum, Rabat

1971–72 'Deliberate Entanglements', University of California Galleries, Los Angeles 'Douze Ans d'Art Contemporain en France', Grand Palais, Paris

1974 Retrospective Exhibition, Stedelijk Museum, Amsterdam. Musée de Nantes

1975 Galerie Alice Pauli, Lausanne Tapisseries Nouvelles, Musée des Arts Decoratifs, Paris

Work included in the following collections

The Museum of Modern Art, New York City
The Museum of Contemporary Crafts, New York City
Cooper-Hewitt Museum, New York City
The Art Institute of Chicago
The Kunstgewebemuseum, Stuttgart
The Landesmuseum, Oldenburg
The Kunstgewebemuseum, Zurich
The Museum of Decorative Arts, Prague
Stedelijk Museum, Amsterdam
Museum of Decorative Arts, Nantes
Ford Foundation Building, New York
Galveston, Texas, Life Insurance Building
Rothschild Bank, Paris
C.B.S., New York
T.W.A., Kennedy Airport, New York
Air France 747 Aircraft
Hotel Camino Reale, Mexico
Georg Jensen Centre for Advanced Design, New York

Ritzi and Peter Jacobi

Biographical details

1935 Peter born in Ploesti (Roumania)

1941 Ritzi born in Bucharest Both study at the Institul de Arte Plastica in Bucharest

1954–61 Peter studies sculpture

1960–67 Ritzi studies tapestry weaving techniques, painting and drawing

1966 They marry and continue to work in their own medium for one year

1967 Begin to work together in tapestry, merging ideas and techniques. Travel to the United States, Scandinavia, Yugoslavia, Egypt, Poland, Russia

1970 Move to Germany, where they establish an atelier in Neubärental, in the Black Forest

Some important exhibitions

1962–68 Individual one-man exhibitions in Roumania

1969, 71, 73, Biennale de la Tapisserie Contemporaine, 75 Lausanne.

1970 Ruth Kaufmann Gallery, New York City

1971 'Deliberate Entanglements', University of California Galleries, Los Angeles

1972 Exhibits in U.S.A., Germany, France and Britain

1974 'In Praise of Hands', Ontario Science Centre, Toronto

1975 Exhibitions in Germany, France and U.S.A.

1976 Retrospective exhibition, Kunsthalle, Mannheim

Work included in the following collections

National Galerie, Bucharest
Museum Craiova
Museum Galati
Museum Constanta
Museum des XX Jahrhundert, Vienna
Museum der Stadt Bochum
Museum für Kunst und Gewerbe, Hamburg
Museum der Stadt Witten
Ostdeutsche Galerie, Regensburg
Galleria Nazionale, Museo di Arte Moderna, Rome
The Power Gallery of Contemporary Art, Sydney
Centre International de la Tapisserie Ancienne Moderne, Lausanne
Sammlung Jacques Lassaing, Paris
Sammlung René Berger, Lausanne
Dreyfus Corporation, New York
Sammlung Hurschler, Pasadena
Sammlung Stadt Frankfurt/Main

Gerhardt Knodel

Biographical details

1940 Born in Milwaukee, Wisconsin

1957–62 Studies at Los Angeles City College and at University of California at Los Angeles under Bernard Kester Bachelor of Arts Degree Instructor of Art at Los Angeles City Schools

1964–72 Study of historic and contemporary fabrics in Europe (England, France, Italy, Greece, Turkey) and at Los Angeles County Art Museum

1968–70 Studies at California State College, Long Beach M.A. Degree in Textiles Lecturer in Fabric

Design at C.S.C. Long Beach Moves to
Cranbrook, Michigan, where is appointed Head of
Fabric Design Department at the Academy of Art

1973–74 Studies historic textiles in India

Some important exhibitions

1960 California State Exhibition (Purchase Award)

1962 'Young Americans', Museum of Contemporary
Crafts, New York

1969 Invitational Fabric and Metal Exhibition,
University of Georgia

1970 'Enclosures' an exhibition of Environments,
California State College at Long Beach
One-man exhibition, Cranbrook Academy of Art

1971–74 Exhibits widely throughout the United States

1975 7e Biennale de la Tapisserie Contemporaine,
Lausanne

Walter Nottingham

Biographical details

1930 Born in Great Falls, Montana

1956–59 Studies at St Cloud State College, Minnesota B.A.
and M.A. Degrees in Textiles

1962 Associate Professor in Textile Department,
University of Wisconsin at River Falls Further
studies at Haystack School of Crafts in Maine

1968 Cranbrook Academy of Arts, Michigan M.A. in
Fine Arts

Some important exhibitions

1966 'Contemporary Weaving' at Fullerton, California

1968 'Wall Hangings', Museum of Modern Art, New
York

1969 'Objects: U.S.A.' Washington D.C.

1970 Jack Larsen Gallery, New York

1971 'Deliberate Entanglements', Los Angeles,
California 5th Biennale de la Tapisserie
Contemporaine, Lausanne

1973 'Creative America', Tokyo

1974 '1st International Exhibition of Miniature Textiles,
British Crafts Centre, London
Minnesota Museum of Art

1974–75 'International Weaving' Govett-Brewster Galleries,
New Zealand and Australia

Wojciech Sadley

Biographical details

1932 Born in Lublin, Poland

1949–59 Studies at the Academy of Fine Arts in
Warsaw Diploma in Interior Architecture
(1954) Diploma in Painting (1959) Studies Music
at the Conservatoire

1959–67 Scientific research at the Institute of Industrial
Design in Warsaw, specialising in Light and
Colour

1967– Appointed Assistant Professor in the Department
of Painting at the Academy of Fine Arts in
Warsaw, with special responsibility for
experimental textile art

Some important exhibitions

1964–65 'Polish Contemporary Textile Art', a travelling
exhibition in Germany, Switzerland and Holland

1963, 65, 67, Biennale Internationale de la Tapisserie
69, 71, 73 Contemporaine, Lausanne

1964, 1969 Biennale, São Paulo, Brazil

1968 Ermitage, Leningrad. Museum of Modern Art,
New York

1969 Stedelijk Museum, Amsterdam
'100 Years of Polish Art', London

1972 Polish Exhibition of Contemporary Art, Paris

1973 Museum Bellerive, Zurich

1974 Arras Gallery, New York

1974, 76 International Exhibition of Miniature Textiles,
British Crafts Centre, London

Work included in the following collections

The National Museum, Warsaw

The Museum, Bydgoszcz

Museum of Textile Industry History, Lodz

Various museums in Sweden, Finland, Norway, Belgium, France,
Switzerland, Holland, Denmark, Canada, United States, German
Federal Republic, Japan

Ceramic frescoes, Coal Mines of Silesia

International Committee of Peace, Helsinki

National Theatre, Warsaw

Moik Schiele

Biographical details

1938 Born in Zurich

1957–61 Studies Textiles under Elsi Giauque at the Zurich
Kunstgewerbeschule. Diploma in Textiles

1959–61, 69 Awarded the Eidenössisches Scholarship and other
prizes

1961 Establishes her own studio in Zurich

1969 Begins exhibiting her work in the United States

1970 Pro Helvetia award

1972 Kantonales Scholarship

Some important exhibitions

1959 'Bildteppiche', Kunstmuseum, St Gallen

1965 'Textile-Elemente', Jürg Bally Galerie, Zurich

1969, 71, 73, Biennale Internationale de la Tapisserie
75 Contemporaine, Lausanne

1969 'Wall Hangings', Museum of Modern Art, New
York

1970 'Moik Schiele', J L Larsen Inc., New York

1971 'Tapisseries Nouvelles' La Galerie du Guet,
Lausanne

1973 'Moik Schiele' at Ruth Kaufmann Gallery, New
York

1974 'Textile Strukturen' Museum Bellerive, Zurich 'In
Praise of Hands' Ontario Science Centre, Toronto

1974, 76 'International Exhibition of Miniature Textiles',
British Crafts Centre, London

Work included in the following collections

Landesmuseum, Oldenburg, Germany

Bellerive Museum, Zurich

Abdankungskapelle Ütliberg, Zurich

Katholische Kirche Urdorf, Zurich

Katholische Kirche Witikon, Zurich
Reformierte Kirche Neu-Affoltern
Stadtspital Bombach, Zurich
Stadtspital Triemli, Zurich
Schulhaus Langnau, Kanton Zurich
Schulhaus Efretikon, Kanton Zurich
Schulhaus Uitikon, Kanton Zurich
Bank of Fort Worth, Fort Worth, Texas
First National Bank of Chicago, Chicago
Hotel Nova Park, Zurich
Geroldswil Gemeindezentrum, Kanton Zurich
Museum of Modern Art, New York

Kay Sekimachi

Biographical details

1926 Born in S. Francisco of Japanese parents; was brought up in the Japanese tradition

1946–49 Studies at the California College of Arts and Crafts: painting and design, then weaving under Trude Guermonprez

1950–56 Begins her career as a weaver, specializing in fibre, yarn and textile techniques, and winning many important awards

1956–58 Works under Jack Lenor Larsen at Haystack Mountain School, Maine

1958–73 Teaches at Summer schools, at Berkeley Adult School (from 1964) and, from 1965 to date, at San Francisco Community College

Some important exhibitions

1960–61 'U.S.I.A. Travelling Exhibition', Europe

1962–63 'Modern American Wall Hangings', Victoria and Albert Museum, London

1968 'Wall Hangings', Museum of Modern Art, New York

1971 'Deliberate Entanglements', University of California, Los Angeles

1973 6th Biennale International de la Tapisserie Contemporaine, Lausanne

1974 'Three Dimensional Fiber', Govett-Brewster Art Gallery, New Plymouth, New Zealand

1974, 76 'International Exhibition of Miniature Textiles', British Crafts Centre, London

Work included in the following collections
Japan Air Lines, San Francisco
Oakland Art Museum
St Paul Art Center, St Paul, Minnesota
San Francisco State College
San Francisco Art Commission
Illinois State University, Normal, Illinois
'Objects: U.S.A.', The Johnson Wax Collection
Dreyfus Fund Collection, New York
'Metromedia', Los Angeles
Smithsonian Institution, Washington D.C.
The Royal Scottish Museum, Edinburgh, Scotland

Sherri Smith

Biographical details

1943 Born in Chicago

1965 B.A. (Art) Hons. at Stanford University

1967 M.F.A. (Weaving and Textile Design) at Cranbrook Academy of Art

1967–71 Works as a textile designer for industry in the Dorothy Liebes Studio in New York, and subsequently as Head of Woven Design Department, Boris Knoll Fabrics, New York City

1970 Receives the 'Young Americans Fellowship Grant' from the American Craft Council

1973 Leads a workshop: 'Multiharness weaving and loom controlled open weaves' at the American Crafts Council Conference, University of Iowa

1971–74 Instructor of Weaving and Textile Design, Colorado State University

1974– Assistant Professor, Weaving and Textile Design, at the School of Art, University of Michigan, Ann Arbor

Some important exhibitions

1968–69 'Wall Hangings' Museum of Modern Art, New York

1969–71 'Young Americans', Museum of Contemporary Crafts, New York

1971, 73, 75 'Biennale Internationale de la Tapisserie Contemporaine', Lausanne

1972 'Fabrications', Cranbrook Academy of Art, Michigan

1973, 74 'New Concepts in Tapestry', Jacques Baruch Gallery, Chicago

1974 'Three Dimensional Fibre', Govett-Brewster Art Gallery, New Plymouth, New Zealand

Inge Vahle

Biographical details

1915 Born in Krevese in the Altmark region of Germany

1934–35 Studies painting at the Academy of Art, Berlin

1935–38 Studies painting at the State Academy of Art, Düsseldorf

1956– Working in Darmstadt

Some important exhibitions

1954, 57 Triennale in Milan (with Fritz Vahle)

1965, 71, 73 'Biennale Internationale de la Tapisserie Contemporaine', Lausanne

1968 Kunsthalle, Darmstadt

1969 International Tapestry Exhibition, Prague

1970 Academy of Fine Arts, Antwerp

1971 Kunsthalle, Mannheim

1974 '1st International Exhibition of Miniature Textiles', British Craft Centre, London

1974 Joseph Magnin Gallery, Denver, Colorado

1974 Jaques Baruch Gallery, Chicago

Work included in the following collections
Centre Allemand, Paris
Deutsches Kulturinstitut, Lissabon
Museen Darmstadt-Hagen-Bonn
Stadthalle Göttingen
Justus-Liebig-Haus, Darmstadt
Universität, Tübingen
Studentenhaus, Konstanz
Stephanuskirche, Gelsenkirchen-Buer